easy
food

photography by Jean Cazals

SILVERBACK

First published in 2004 by
Quadrille Publishing Limited
Alhambra House
27-31 Charing Cross Road
London WC2H OLS

This edition published by Silverback Books, Inc.
San Francisco
California
www.silverbackbooks.com

ISBN 1-59637-007-6

Creative Director Helen Lewis
Editorial Director Jane O'Shea
Consultant Editor Janet Illsley
Photographic Direction Vanessa Courtier
Senior Designer Jim Smith
Designer Ros Holder
Editor Jane Keskeys
Production Beverley Richardson

Printed in China

Cookery notes
All recipes serve 4 unless otherwise stated. All spoon measures are level
unless otherwise indicated. Follow either metric or imperial measures, not a
mixture of both as they are not necessarily interchangeable. Use fresh herbs
and freshly ground black pepper unless otherwise suggested.

Contents

easy soups and snacks

Mediterranean fish soup

Serves 4–6

2 pounds mixed fish, such as
   monkfish, red mullet and
   mackerel, cleaned
8 ounces raw tiger shrimp
6 tablespoons extra-virgin olive oil
2 red onions, roughly chopped
2 garlic cloves, crushed
2 carrots, diced
1 celery stick, diced
4 tablespoons brandy
5 cups water
15-ounce can chopped tomatoes
4 fresh rosemary sprigs
2 fresh bay leaves
¼ teaspoon saffron strands
salt and pepper
For the Parmesan chips
4 ounces Parmesan cheese, freshly
   grated
To finish
4–6 tablespoons crème fraîche
   (optional)
paprika, for sprinkling

1 Preheat oven to 400°F. Wash and dry the fish and cut into chunks, discarding the heads. Devein the shrimp, and rinse well.

2 Heat 3 tablespoons of oil in a skillet, and fry the fish chunks and shrimp over a high heat until golden. Using a slotted spoon, transfer to a saucepan.

3 Heat the remaining oil. Add the onions, garlic, carrots, and celery, and fry gently for 10 minutes. Pour in the brandy and let bubble until evaporated.

4 Add the sautéed vegetables to the fish, with the water, tomatoes, herbs, and saffron. Slowly bring to the boil, then cover and simmer for 30 minutes.

5 Meanwhile, make the Parmesan chips. Sprinkle 4 small circles of grated cheese on a well oiled nonstick baking sheet. Bake for 3–4 minutes until crisp and golden. Leave on the baking sheet for 5 minutes, then carefully peel off, using a spatula. Repeat to make 16 chips in total.

6 Purée the soup, including the seafood, in a blender or food processor until smooth. Pass through a fine sieve into a clean pan. Season and heat through.

7 Ladle the soup into warmed bowls. Drizzle with crème fraîche, if wished, and sprinkle with paprika. Serve with the Parmesan chips.

Parmesan chips give this version of a classic soupe de poisson a new twist.

Chilled tomato soup with Thai flavors

Serves 6

1½ pound ripe tomatoes

2 garlic cloves, crushed

1 teaspoon grated fresh gingerroot

4 lime leaves, shredded

2–4 red chiles, seeded and diced

2 green onions, trimmed and chopped

2 tablespoons chopped fresh cilantro

1¼ cup iced water

1¼ cup tomato juice

2 tablespoons light soy sauce

2 tablespoons rice wine vinegar

1 tablespoon sesame oil

salt and pepper

To serve

ice cubes

torn cilantro leaves

sesame oil

1 Roughly chop the tomatoes and place in a blender with the garlic, ginger, lime leaves, chiles, green onions, and cilantro. Purée until fairly smooth.

2 Transfer to a large bowl and whisk in the water, tomato juice, soy sauce, wine vinegar, and sesame oil. Season with salt and pepper to taste. Cover and chill in the refrigerator for several hours.

3 Serve with ice cubes, garnished with coriander and a drizzle of sesame oil.

This adaptation of the classic Spanish gazpacho uses Thai ingredients. It is best appreciated during the summer months, when the heat demands a cooling starter and tomatoes are full of flavor.

Pea soup with minted gremolata

Illustrated on previous pages

2 tablespoons butter
1 onion, diced
1 potato, peeled and diced
1 pound shelled fresh peas
 (see note)
3 cups vegetable or chicken stock
2 fresh mint sprigs
salt and pepper

For the gremolata
2 tablespoons shredded fresh mint
 leaves
grated rind of 1–2 lemons
1 garlic clove, crushed
To serve
extra-virgin olive oil

1 Melt the butter in a pan, add the onion and potato, and fry gently for 10 minutes until softened and lightly golden. Add the peas, stock, mint, and seasoning. Bring to the boil, lower the heat, cover, and simmer gently for 20 minutes.
2 Meanwhile, mix the gremolata ingredients together in a bowl.
3 Transfer the soup to a blender, and purée until very smooth. Return to the pan and heat through. Adjust the seasoning to taste.
4 Spoon the soup into warm bowls and serve topped with the gremolata and a drizzle of olive oil.

Note Use frozen peas when fresh ones are out of season.

Gremolata—an Italian mix of mint, lemon zest, and garlic—adds a real zing to this creamy, fresh-tasting soup.

Fennel broth with anchovy croûtes

Serves 6

2 tablespoons olive oil

1 onion, sliced

4 garlic cloves, crushed

grated rind of ½ orange

1 tablespoon chopped fresh thyme

2 fennel bulbs, thinly sliced

2 tablespoons Pernod

15-ounce can chopped tomatoes

3¾ cups fish stock

For the croûtes

6 thin slices French bread

2-ounce can anchovy fillets, drained
  and chopped

¼ cup pine nuts

1 garlic clove, crushed

2 teaspoons lemon juice

pepper

To finish

4 tablespoons crème fraîche

fennel fronds or dill, to garnish

1 Preheat oven to 400°F. Heat the olive oil in a saucepan, add the onion, garlic, orange rind, thyme, and fennel, and fry gently for 10 minutes until the onion is softened and lightly golden. Add the Pernod and allow to bubble until it is evaporated.

2 Add the chopped tomatoes and stock, bring to the boil, cover, and simmer gently for 30 minutes.

3 Meanwhile make the croûtes. Put the slices of French bread on a baking sheet and bake for 10 minutes until crisp and golden. Set aside.

4 Put the anchovy fillets, pine nuts, garlic, lemon juice, and pepper in a blender or food processor, and purée until fairly smooth. Spread the anchovy paste on top of the croûtes.

5 Spoon the fennel soup into warmed bowls, and top each serving with an anchovy croûte. Add a spoonful of crème fraîche, and garnish with a sprinkling of chopped fennel fronds or dill.

A fragrant fennel and fish broth topped with savory anchovy croûtes.

Roasted tomato soup with ricotta

Serves 6
8 tablespoons olive oil
1 onion, finely chopped
2 pounds ripe tomatoes, halved
12 garlic cloves, peeled
handful fresh mint leaves
1 teaspoon superfine sugar
salt and pepper

2½ cups vegetable stock
¾ cup dried pastina (small soup pasta)
For the garnish
2 ounces ricotta cheese, crumbled
mint leaves
olive oil, to drizzle

1 Preheat oven to 425°F. Heat half the oil in a shallow flameproof casserole, and fry the onion for 10 minutes. Add the tomatoes, garlic cloves, mint, sugar, salt, and pepper. Bring to the boil.

2 Transfer to the oven, and roast, uncovered, for 20 minutes. Let cool slightly, then purée the tomato mixture with the remaining oil in a blender or food processor; return to the pan.

3 Stir in the stock and bring to the boil. Add the pasta and simmer gently for 10 minutes until al dente. Adjust the seasoning to taste.

4 Spoon into warmed bowls and top with crumbled ricotta, mint leaves, and a generous drizzling of olive oil. Serve with Italian bread.

Roasted tomatoes give this hearty Italian tomato soup a great depth of flavor.

Mixed vegetable sushi

Illustrated on previous pages

1 cup sushi rice
3 tablespoons rice wine vinegar
2 tablespoons superfine sugar
salt and pepper
2 eggs, lightly beaten
a little sunflower oil
8 sheets nori seaweed

generous 1 cup mixed vegetables,
including carrot, cucumber, and
cooked baby corn, cut into strips
To serve
wasabi paste
pickled ginger
Japanese soy sauce

1 Cook rice according to pack instructions.

2 Warm the vinegar, sugar, and 1½ teaspoon salt together in a small pan until they have dissolved.

3 Transfer the rice to a bowl and stir in the vinegar. Cover with a dish towel; let cool.

4 In another bowl, beat the eggs with a little salt and pepper. Brush an omelet pan with a little oil. Heat gently, pour in the egg, and cook for 2 minutes until set. Cool, then cut into strips the same size as the vegetables.

5 Lay 1 sheet of seaweed on a bamboo mat or board, and trim off the top third. Spread about ⅙ cup rice along the front end, flatten slightly, then place a line of omelet and vegetable strips on top. Roll up tightly to form a log. Cut into 5 or 6 slices.

6 Repeat with the remaining rice and vegetable strips to make a selection of different sushi fillings.

7 Arrange the sushi in individual bowls. Serve accompanied by the wasabi, pickled ginger, and soy sauce.

The ingredients are available from larger supermarkets and oriental food stores, so it's surprisingly easy to make your own sushi.

Roasted tomatoes on chickpea cakes

Serves 6
¾ cup (chickpea) flour
1 teaspoon salt
2 cups cold water
3 tbsp olive oil, plus extra for frying
24 large cherry tomatoes

1 garlic clove, crushed
4 fresh thyme sprigs
pinch of sugar
salt and pepper
1 tablespoon balsamic vinegar
extra-virgin olive oil, to serve

1 Preheat oven to 450°F. Sift the flour and salt into a bowl. Gradually whisk in the water with 1 tablespoon olive oil until smooth.
2 Turn into a nonstick pan and slowly bring to the boil, stirring constantly until the mixture is thickened enough to leave the side of the pan. Spoon into an oiled 9–inch shallow cake pan. Set aside to cool.
3 Put the tomatoes, garlic, thyme, and sugar in a small roasting pan; season with salt and pepper. Drizzle with remaining oil and roast for 20 minutes until softened. Sprinkle with the balsamic vinegar.
4 Turn out the chickpea "cake" and cut into 6 wedges. Heat a little oil in a large skillet and fry the chickpea wedges for 1–2 minutes each side until golden. Serve the chickpea wedges topped with the tomatoes and their juices and a generous drizzle of extra-virgin olive oil.

Similar to set polenta but with a smoother texture, chickpea wedges are the ideal base for juicy, roasted tomatoes.

Piadina with trout and aioli

Serves 6

For the piadina

1⅝ cups all-purpose flour

salt and pepper

1 tablespoon butter

⅝ cup warm water

For the aioli

2 egg yolks

1 tablespoon lemon juice

1¼ cups olive oil

2 garlic cloves, crushed

For the topping

2 tablespoons extra-virgin olive oil

6 trout fillets

squeeze of lemon juice

few arugula leaves

1 Sift the flour and ½ teaspoon salt into a bowl, rub in the butter, then work in the water to form a soft dough. Knead for 10 minutes on a lightly floured surface until smooth. Wrap in plastic wrap and rest for 30 minutes.

2 To make the aioli, put the egg yolks, lemon juice, and seasoning in a food processor and pulse briefly. With the motor still running, slowly add the oil through the funnel until glossy and thick. Turn into a bowl; stir in the garlic.

3 Divide dough into 6 pieces. Roll out on a floured surface to 7-inch rounds. Preheat a griddle or heavy skillet and fry the breads, one at a time, for 1 minute. Turn and cook underside for 30 seconds; keep warm.

4 Heat the oil in a skillet and cook the fish fillets for 1–2 minutes each side. Season and flavor with a little lemon juice.

5 Top each piadina with 1 trout fillet, a spoonful of aioli, and a few arugula leaves. Serve at once.

Piadina are Italian flat griddle breads, often served with a topping. Make them in advance and reheat in the oven.

Smoked fish tartlets

Serves 8

1 pound ready-made shortcrust
  pastry
1 pound smoked trout, skinned
⅔ cup milk
2 strips of lemon zest
⅔ cup heavy cream

2 medium eggs, lightly beaten
1 tablespoon chopped fresh tarragon
pinch of cayenne pepper
salt and pepper
tarragon leaves, to garnish
salad leaves, to serve

1 Preheat oven to 350°F. Divide the pastry into 8 pieces. Roll out on a lightly floured surface into thin rounds and use to line eight 4-inch individual quiche pans. Prick the bases with a fork. Chill in the refrigerator for 30 minutes.
2 Line the pastry cases with waxed paper and baking beans and bake blind for 15 minutes; remove the paper and beans and bake for another 10–15 minutes until the pastry is crisp and golden. Set aside to cool.
3 Place the fish in a shallow pan with the milk and lemon strips. Bring to a gentle simmer, cover, and poach gently for 7 minutes. Cool slightly, then flake the fish, discarding any bones. Leave to cool.
4 Put the fish in a bowl with the cream, eggs, tarragon, cayenne, and salt and pepper. Stir gently to mix.
5 Spoon the filling into the flan cases and bake for 25 minutes until risen and set. Leave to cool slightly for a few minutes. Serve warm on a bed of mixed salad leaves, garnished with tarragon sprigs.

Smoked fish works beautifully in these melt-in-the-mouth tartlets.

Smoked chicken and sweet onion wrap

1 tablespoon olive oil
1 large red onion, sliced
1 red chile, seeded and sliced
½ teaspoon salt
3 tablespoons redcurrant jelly
1 tablespoon red wine vinegar
4 large flour tortillas

mizuna or other salad leaves
½ pound smoked chicken (or cooked breast fillet), shredded
1 small ripe avocado, peeled, stoned and sliced
4 tablespoons crème fraîche

1 Heat the oil in a skillet, add the onion and chile and fry over a medium heat for 10 minutes until browned. Add the salt, redcurrant jelly, vinegar, and 1 tablespoon water; cook gently for another 15 minutes until thickened. Leave to cool.

2 Lay the tortillas flat and then top each one with a few salad leaves, the shredded chicken, avocado slices, a spoonful of the onion jam, and a dollop of crème fraîche.

3 Carefully fold the tortilla around the filling to form a cone shape, and wrap up firmly. Serve at once, or wrap securely in napkins or waxed paper and keep in a cool place until ready to serve.

The sandwich of the moment, the "wrap" is simply a tasty filling wrapped up in a soft flour tortilla.

Roasted chicken and spinach wrap

8 ounces roasted chicken (off the
  bone)
4 large flour tortillas
2 ounces young spinach leaves,
  stems removed
2 fresh peaches, halved, stoned, and
  sliced

2 tablespoons mayonnaise
2 teaspoons chopped fresh basil
freshly grated Parmesan, to taste

1 Cut the roast chicken into long, thin shreds.
2 Lay the tortillas flat on a clean surface and top each one with a handful of
spinach leaves. Scatter the shredded chicken and peach slices over.
3 Mix the mayonnaise with the chopped basil and spoon on top of the
chicken. Grate fresh Parmesan over, to taste.
4 Carefully fold the tortilla around the filling to form a cone shape and wrap
up firmly. Serve at once, or wrap securely in waxed paper and keep in a cool
place until ready to serve.

Flour tortillas wrapped around a filling of
shredded chicken, tender spinach, peach
slices, and chopped basil for a portable snack.

Pork and liver pâté with apple relish

¼ pound chicken livers, diced

3 tablespoons marsala

1½ sticks (12 tablespoons) unsalted butter

3 shallots, finely chopped

2 garlic cloves, crushed

1 tablespoon chopped fresh sage

¼ teaspoon cayenne pepper

½ cup pork or chicken stock

1 cup fresh breadcrumbs

1 cup cooked pork, diced

½ cup cooked ham, diced

salt and pepper

1 fresh sage sprig

For the apple relish

1 small onion, sliced

½ teaspoon grated fresh gingerroot

1 large cooking apple, peeled, cored, and diced

4 tablespoons cider vinegar

4 tablespoons water

5 tablespoons light muscovado sugar

1 Put the chicken livers and marsala in a bowl, and leave to marinate for at least 15 minutes.

2 Melt 4 tablespoons of the butter in a skillet, add the shallots, garlic, and sage, and fry gently for 5 minutes. Add the chicken livers and marsala. Fry over a high heat for 1 minute, then stir in the cayenne and stock. Simmer for 3–4 minutes until the livers are cooked. Leave to cool completely.

3 Put the cooled mixture in a food processor with the breadcrumbs, pork, and ham; work briefly to chop finely. Season to taste.

4 Spoon the mixture into a pâté dish and smooth the surface. Melt remaining butter over a low heat, let cool for 5 minutes, then carefully pour over the pâté. Position the sage sprig on top, pressing gently down into the butter. Chill for several hours.

5 Meanwhile, make the relish. Put all the ingredients in a pan and bring to the boil. Lower heat and simmer for 35–40 minutes until thickened. Cool and season to taste.

6 Serve the pâté with the relish and crisp French sticks.

A simple pâté set under a layer of butter, served with a tangy apple and ginger relish.

Bresaola antipasto

Illustrated on previous pages

⅜ cup good-quality, large salted
   capers
1 tablespoon all-purpose flour
3 tablespoons olive oil
3 tablespoons fresh parsley leaves
squeeze of lemon juice
16 slices good-quality bresaola
3 ounces mixed mâche and arugula
   leaves
¼ cup pecorino cheese shavings

For the dressing
½ small shallot, finely chopped
1 teaspoon white wine vinegar
½ teaspoon Dijon mustard
½ teaspoon sugar
4 tablespoons extra-virgin olive oil
salt and pepper

1 Soak the capers in cold water for 30 minutes. Drain and pat dry with
paper towels, then dust with the flour.
2 Heat the oil in a small skillet, and fry the capers for 2–3 minutes
until crisp and golden. Add the parsley leaves and fry for 30 seconds.
Drain on paper towels, then toss the mixture with the lemon juice.
3 Whisk the dressing ingredients together in a bowl.
4 Arrange the bresaola on serving plates. Top with the salad leaves, caper
mixture, and pecorino shavings. Drizzle with the dressing and serve.

Cured beef, crisp capers, and sweet/sharp
pecorino cheese combine beautifully in this
Italian appetizer.

Smoked duck antipasto

1 large smoked duck breast
3 ounces mizuna or arugula leaves
2 ounces bean sprouts
handful of cilantro leaves
2 teaspoons toasted sesame seeds

For the dressing
2 tablespoons sunflower oil
½ teaspoon sesame oil
1 tablespoon lime juice
1½ teaspoon superfine sugar
1 red chile, seeded and chopped
salt

1 Thinly slice the duck breast, and arrange on individual serving plates.
2 Top each serving with a handful of mizuna or arugula leaves, bean sprouts, a few cilantro leaves, and a sprinkling of toasted sesame seeds.
3 For the dressing, whizz together the sunflower oil, sesame oil, lime juice, caster sugar, red chile, and a pinch of salt.
4 Drizzle the dressing over the salads to serve.

Note If you are unable to buy whole smoked duck breast, look for a pack of sliced smoked duck breast in the supermarket chilled cabinet.

Cilantro, beansprouts, chile, and sesame flavors give this unusual antipasto an oriental twist.

Mini chicken kiev

Serves 2

2 large skinless chicken breast fillets
4 tablespoons seasoned flour
1 large egg, lightly beaten
1 cup dried white breadcrumbs
1 tablespoon sesame seeds
sunflower oil, for shallow frying

For the spiced butter

4 tablespoons butter, at room
  temperature
1 small red chile, seeded, and diced
½ teaspoon ground cumin
1 tablespoon chopped fresh cilantro
grated rind and juice of ½ lime
salt and pepper

To serve

lime wedges

1 Start by making the spiced butter. Place all the ingredients in a bowl and beat until well blended. Roll into a small log, wrap in foil, and freeze for at least 1 hour.

2 Lay each chicken breast flat and slice in half horizontally to give 4 thin escalopes. Place between sheets of plastic wrap, and beat flat with a rolling pin.

3 Cut the chilled butter into 4 slices. Place 1 slice in the middle of each escalope and fold the chicken over the butter to enclose and seal. Secure with toothpicks.

4 Dust each parcel with flour, then dip into the egg. Mix the breadcrumbs and sesame seeds together. Carefully toss the chicken parcels in the crumb mixture and coat well. Chill for several hours, or overnight.

5 Heat a shallow layer of oil in a skillet and gently fry the parcels for 15–20 minutes, turning several times, to brown evenly. Drain on paper towels, and remove the toothpicks. Serve with lime wedges.

Serve these croquettes as a snack lunch or supper with a crisp salad.

Chicken liver and blueberry salad

4 tablespoons extra virgin olive oil
⅗ cup whole unblanched almonds
coarse salt and pepper
¾ pound chicken livers, halved
   if large
1⅓ cup blueberries

1 tablespoon raspberry vinegar
¼ pound mixed salad leaves
2 ounces green beans, blanched
few fresh herb leaves (e.g. basil,
   mint, parsley)

1 Heat 2 tablespoons oil in a skillet and fry the almonds gently until evenly browned. Remove with a slotted spoon, dust with coarse salt, and set aside.
2 Increase the heat. Add the chicken livers to the pan and fry for 1 minute. Turn and fry for another 1 minute until browned on the outside, but still slightly pink in the middle. Remove and let rest for a few minutes.
3 Return the pan to the heat, add the blueberries, and warm through for 30 seconds. Remove from the heat and add the remaining oil and the raspberry vinegar.
4 Arrange the salad leaves, beans, herbs, and almonds on serving plates. Add the chicken livers, then spoon the blueberries and pan juices over. Serve at once, with warm bread.

Blueberries and a warm, fruity dressing perfectly offset rich chicken livers.

easy
pasta

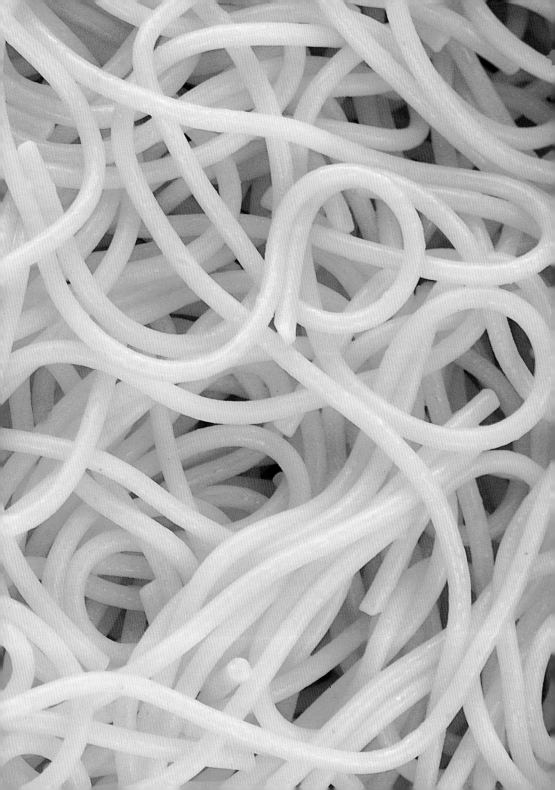

Pasta with chile pesto

1 large red bell pepper
3 handfuls fresh basil leaves
1 garlic clove, crushed
2 ripe tomatoes, skinned
2 tablespoons pine nuts
3 tablespoons sun-dried tomato paste
3 tablespoons tomato paste

1 teaspoon mild chile powder
few drops of Tabasco sauce
2 ounces Parmesan cheese, freshly
  grated
⅝ cup light olive oil
1 pound dried casarecce or spaghetti

1 Grill the pepper, turning occasionally, until charred. Cool slightly, then skin, halve, and de-seed. Place in a food processor with the other ingredients, except the oil and pasta. Process until almost smooth. Turn into a bowl and stir in the oil.

2 Bring a large pan of salted water to the boil. Then add the pasta and cook until al dente.

3 Drain the pasta, keeping back 2 tablespoons water in the pan. Immediately toss with chile pesto to taste, allowing approximately 2 tablespoons per serving.

Note Holding back a few tablespoonfuls of the cooking water with the pasta helps the sauce to cling to the pasta and adds a certain creaminess.

This robust pasta dish is spiked with a fiery homemade chile pesto—to delicious effect. Store any leftover pesto in a jar, covered with a layer of olive oil, in the fridge for up to 2 weeks. It is excellent with broiled chicken.

Fusilli with tomatoes and mozzarella

1 pound 2 ounces plum tomatoes,
    roughly chopped
1 garlic clove, crushed
2 tablespoons chopped fresh basil
2 teaspoons chopped fresh marjoram
4 anchovy fillets, finely chopped

juice of ½ lemon
4 tablespoons extra-virgin olive oil
salt and pepper
1 pound dried tricolore fusilli or
    pasta shells
¾ pound mozzarella cheese, diced

1 Place the chopped tomatoes, garlic, herbs, anchovies, lemon juice, and olive oil in a bowl. Season with pepper and a little salt, toss to mix; set aside.
2 Cook the pasta in a large pan of boiling salted water, until al dente.
3 Drain the pasta, and place in a warm serving bowl. Immediately add the mozzarella, and toss to melt slightly, then add the tomato sauce, and toss well. Check the seasoning, and serve at once.

Tricolore pasta with a sauce of plum tomatoes, marjoram, basil, anchovies, and mozzarella.

Fettucine with vegetable julienne

2½ cups homemade or bought fresh
chicken stock

7 ounces carrots, cut into julienne
strips

7 ounces leeks, cut into julienne
strips

3 tomatoes, skinned, seeded, and
sliced pepper

10 ounces dried fettucine or
tagliatelle

freshly grated Parmesan, to serve
(optional)

1 Bring the chicken stock to the boil in a pan. Add the carrots, and simmer
for about 2 minutes; remove with a slotted spoon, and place in a bowl.
Repeat with the leeks; add to the bowl. Boil the stock to reduce by about half.
2 Cook the pasta in a large pan of boiling salted water, until al dente.
3 Add the leeks, carrots, and tomatoes to the chicken stock, and bring to a
simmer to warm through.
4 Drain the pasta, and add to the vegetable julienne and stock. Serve in
warmed bowls.

For this delicately flavored pasta dish,
vegetable julienne sticks are cooked briefly
in a tasty stock, then combined with noodles.

Corn pasta with fennel and red onion

Illustrated on previous pages

1 fennel bulb, cored and finely diced
1 pound 2 ounces ripe plum
   tomatoes, seeded and finely diced
1 red onion, finely diced
2 tablespoons chopped fresh basil
2 tablespoons chopped fresh dill
3 tablespoons extra-virgin olive oil
juice of 1 lemon

salt and pepper
1 pound dried corn pasta (preferably
   fusilli)
basil leaves and red onion slices, to
   garnish
freshly grated Parmesan cheese, to
   serve

1 In a bowl, mix together the fennel, tomatoes, red onion, herbs, olive
oil, and lemon juice. Season with salt and pepper to taste and set aside.
2 Cook the pasta in a large pan of boiling salted water until al dente.
3 Drain the pasta, and return to the pan. Add the fennel sauce and toss
to mix. Check the seasoning. Cover with a lid and then leave to stand
for 2–3 minutes to allow the flavors to infuse.
4 Serve garnished with basil and red onion slices. Accompany with some
grated Parmesan.

Fresh fennel, dill, red onion, tomatoes, and
herbs give this uncooked sauce a wonderfully
refreshing taste sensation.

Spaghetti with eggplants

Serves 4–6

2 pounds eggplants, cut into
  1cm/½in dice
salt and pepper
5 tablespoons olive oil
2–3 tablespoons crushed sun-dried
  tomatoes in oil

1 tablespoon finely shredded fresh
  basil
1 pound 2 ounces dried spaghetti
¾ cup pine nuts, toasted
freshly grated pecorino or Parmesan
  cheese, to serve

1 Put the eggplants in a colander and sprinkle generously with salt.
Leave to drain for 30 minutes. Rinse well and pat dry on a dish towel.
2 Heat the oil in a pan, and fry the eggplants for about 15 minutes, until
tender and brown. Add the sun-dried tomatoes, basil, and pepper.
3 Meanwhile, cook the spaghetti in a large pan of boiling salted water until
al dente. Drain and toss with the eggplant mixture and pine nuts. Serve
at once, with grated pecorino or Parmesan.

Note It is worth salting the eggplants for this dish, to draw out their
bitter juices.

Serve with an arugula salad.

Pasta with mushroom, thyme, and zucchini

1 pound dried curly pasta shapes, such as spiralli or casarecce, or shells
salt and pepper
¼ cup butter
1 garlic clove, chopped

4–6 large flat mushrooms, sliced
1 tablespoon chopped fresh thyme
4 small zucchini, coarsely grated
pecorino or Parmesan cheese shavings, to serve

1 Bring a large pan of salted water to the boil. Add the pasta and cook until al dente.

2 Meanwhile, melt the butter in a skillet. Add the garlic and cook gently for 2–3 minutes until golden.

3 Add the sliced mushrooms and fry for about 2 minutes until softened and beginning to brown.

4 Stir in the thyme and grated zucchini. Increase the heat, and cook, stirring constantly, for about 5 minutes or until the zucchini are tender. Season with salt and pepper to taste.

5 Drain the pasta, keeping 2 tablespoons water in the pan. Immediately toss the pasta with the sauce and serve topped with pecorino or Parmesan shavings.

Note For speed, use a food processor fitted with a coarse grating disk to prepare the zucchini, or dice them if you prefer.

Variation Use 6 ounces button or chestnut mushrooms instead of flat mushrooms.

Mushrooms and zucchini are perfect partners. Sautéed with garlic and thyme, they make a wonderful aromatic sauce.

Spaghetti, broccoli and garlic breadcrumbs

4 tablespoons butter
2 garlic cloves, crushed
1 cup fresh white breadcrumbs
10 ounces broccoli, divided into
   sprigs
salt and pepper
½ pound dried spaghetti

6 tablespoons extra-virgin olive oil
1 red chile, seeded and diced
juice of ½ lemon
1 tablespoon chopped fresh parsley
freshly grated Parmesan cheese,
   to serve

1 Melt the butter in a large skillet. Add the garlic and breadcrumbs, and stir-fry over a medium heat until golden. Remove and set aside.
2 Blanch the broccoli in boiling water for 2 minutes; drain and refresh under cold water.
3 Add the spaghetti to a large pan of boiling salted water and then cook until al dente.
4 Meanwhile, heat half the oil in a clean skillet, add the chile and broccoli, and stir-fry for 3 minutes until tender. Add the lemon juice, remaining oil, and parsley.
5 Drain the spaghetti, retaining 4 tablespoons cooking water. Add to the broccoli and toss over a low heat for 1 minute. Serve topped with the garlic breadcrumbs and a little grated Parmesan.

Sprouting broccoli is ideal for this simple pasta dish. Otherwise, you can use calabrese, cavolo nero or collard greens.

Spaghetti with leeks and pancetta

Serves 4–6

2 tablespoons olive oil

2 medium leeks, thinly sliced

6 ounces pancetta, thinly sliced

⅜ cup white wine

1¼ cup light cream

1 pound 2 ounces dried spaghetti

3 tablespoons freshly grated
  Parmesan cheese

1 Heat the oil in a pan, and fry the leeks gently for 3–4 minutes to soften. Add the pancetta and cook for 4–5 minutes until beginning to brown.

2 Add the wine, stir to deglaze, and bring nearly to the boil. Add the cream and warm through.

3 Meanwhile, cook the spaghetti in a large pan of boiling salted water until al dente. Drain and toss with the sauce and Parmesan to serve.

This deliciously rich, creamy dish is equally good with tagliatelle or linguine.

Spaghetti with pepper butter sauce

3 large red bell peppers
9 ounces dried spaghetti
salt and pepper
6 tablespoons butter
dash of Tabasco sauce
2 tablespoons chopped fresh basil

4 tablespoons milk
shredded basil leaves, to garnish
freshly grated Parmesan cheese,
  to serve

1 Peel the red peppers, using a potato peeler, then halve and remove the core and seeds. Place the pepper flesh in a food processor and process to a purée.
2 Cook the spaghetti in a large pan of boiling salted water until al dente.
3 Meanwhile, transfer the red pepper purée to a saucepan, and add the butter, Tabasco, chopped basil, and milk. Season generously with salt and pepper. Cover and simmer gently, stirring frequently, for 8–10 minutes.
4 Drain the spaghetti and return to the warm pan. Add the pepper butter sauce and toss to mix.
5 Divide the pasta between warmed serving plates. Sprinkle with basil and serve with grated Parmesan.

Red bell peppers, chopped in a food processor, give this sauce a wonderful silky texture and sweet flavor, while Tabasco adds a touch of heat. Serve with an arugula salad.

Spinach tagliatelle with minted peas

1 pound dried spinach tagliatelle
salt and pepper
6 tablespoons butter
4 green onions, thinly sliced
3½ cups peas (shelled fresh or frozen)
2 tablespoons chopped fresh mint

2 teaspoon finely grated orange rind
1 tablespoon orange juice
freshly grated Parmesan cheese,
  to serve

1 Cook the tagliatelle in a large pan of boiling salted water until al dente.
2 Meanwhile, melt 4 tablespoons of the butter in a pan. Add the green onions and cook gently for 3–4 minutes or until tender.
3 Add the peas and ½ cup oz water; cook for 3–4 minutes or until tender. Stir in the mint.
4 Put the remaining butter, orange rind, and juice in a large, warm serving dish. Drain the pasta and add to the dish with the pea sauce. Toss well and season with salt and pepper to taste.
5 Serve topped with grated Parmesan.

Spinach tagliatelle with green onions, peas, and chopped mint in an orange-butter sauce.

Pasta with avocado and cilantro pesto

2 small, ripe avocados
3 green onions, minced
3 handfuls fresh cilantro leaves
1 tablespoon lime juice
few drops of jalapeno or Tabasco
   sauce

2 tablespoons crème fraîche
1 large tomato, skinned and diced
salt and pepper
1 pound dried buckwheat noodles,
   or wholewheat spaghetti
cilantro leaves, to garnish

1 Halve, stone, and peel the avocados. Put them in a food processor with the green onions, cilantro leaves, lime juice, and jalapeno or Tabasco sauce. Pulse until the ingredients are evenly mixed and finely chopped.
2 Turn into a bowl and stir in the crème fraîche, then the diced tomato. Season with salt and pepper to taste.
3 Bring a large pan of salted water to the boil. Add the noodles or spaghetti and cook until al dente.
4 Drain the pasta, keeping back 2 tablespoons water in the pan. Immediately toss with the sauce, and serve scattered with cilantro leaves.

Note In general, thick sauces are best with chunky pasta, such as spirals, penne, shells, or rigatoni. Soft, fluid sauces suit long pasta, like noodles or spaghetti.

This wonderfully pungent pesto sauce is particularly good with buckwheat noodles.

Penne with roasted beets and feta

1 pound baby beets, trimmed (see note)
1 garlic clove, crushed
2 tablespoons walnut oil, plus extra to drizzle
salt and pepper

10 ounces dried penne or other pasta shapes
50g/2oz arugula leaves
¼ pound feta cheese, crumbled
2 tablespoons toasted pine nuts
pecorino or Parmesan cheese, to serve

1 Preheat oven to 425°F. Put the beets in a small roasting pan with the garlic, oil, salt, and pepper. Add 2 tablespoons water, and roast in the oven for 50–60 minutes until tender. Keep warm.
2 Add the pasta to a large pan of boiling salted water and then cook until al dente.
3 Drain the pasta thoroughly and immediately toss with the arugula leaves, roasted beets, pepper, and a little extra walnut oil.
4 Spoon the pasta mixture into warmed bowls. Scatter the crumbled feta and toasted pine nuts over. Drizzle with walnut oil to serve.

Note To make sure the baby beets are similar in size, halve any larger ones.

Sweet roasted beets and salty feta combine well in this pretty pasta dish. The arugula leaves just wilt as they are stirred into the hot pasta.

Tomato spaghetti with cilantro and avocado

Illustrated on previous pages

1 pound 2 ounces cherry tomatoes, quartered

2 tablespoons torn fresh cilantro leaves

grated rind and juice of ½ lemon

1 garlic clove, crushed

3 tablespoons extra-virgin olive oil

3 small avocados (preferably haas), peeled, stoned and cut into ½-inch cubes

salt and pepper

1 pound dried tomato spaghetti

1 Combine the tomatoes, cilantro, lemon rind and juice, garlic, and olive oil in a large bowl. Add the chopped avocados and toss gently to mix. Season with salt and pepper to taste and set aside.

2 Cook the pasta in a large pan of boiling salted water until al dente.

3 Drain the pasta and toss gently with the sauce to serve.

Note Don't prepare this sauce too far in advance, or the avocado may discolor and spoil the appearance of the dish.

The heat of the cooked spaghetti brings out the full flavors of creamy, ripe avocados and cherry tomatoes.

Buckwheat noodles with savoy cabbage

2 tablespoons olive oil
4 ounces pancetta or lightly smoked
 bacon, diced
2 red onions, sliced
½ small Savoy cabbage, shredded
3 garlic cloves, chopped

8 ounces buckwheat (soba) noodles,
 or egg tagliatelle
salt and pepper
8-ounce tub mascarpone cheese
5 ounces dolcelatte cheese, diced

1 Heat the oil in a large, deep skillet, add the pancetta or bacon and onions, and fry for 5 minutes, stirring occasionally.
2 Stir in the cabbage and garlic, cover, and cook for 8–10 minutes until the cabbage is tender.
3 Meanwhile, cook the noodles in a large pan of boiling salted water until al dente.
4 Drain the noodles thoroughly and toss with the cabbage; season. Add the cheeses and heat gently until they melt to a creamy sauce. Serve immediately.

Japanese noodles tossed with pancetta and cabbage in a creamy cheese sauce.

Spaghetti, peas, and oven-dried tomatoes

Serves 4–6
1 pound 2 ounces dried spaghetti
salt and pepper
1 pound frozen or fresh peas or
  petits pois

1 batch oven-dried tomatoes
  (see below)
2 tablespoons finely shredded fresh
  mint

1 Cook the spaghetti in a large pan of boiling salted water until al dente.
2 Meanwhile, cook the peas in a separate pan of boiling water until tender.
3 Drain the pasta and peas, return to the warm pasta pan and add the oven-dried tomatoes with 2–3 tbsp of the oil, and the mint. Toss lightly, season, and serve.

Oven-dried tomatoes Preheat oven to 250°F. Lay 14 ounces halved cherry tomatoes on a nonstick baking tray, cut side up. Sprinkle with salt, pepper, and sugar. Bake for 1½ hours or until dry but not brown. Cool slightly, then put into a bowl and add extra-virgin olive oil to cover. When cold, store in jars covered with a layer of olive oil. Use as required.

Oven-dried cherry tomatoes bring a sweet intensity to this dish.

Tagliatelle with wild mushroom sauce

¾ ounce dried porcini mushrooms
⅝ cup dry white wine
3 garlic cloves, peeled
1¼ cup heavy cream
½ cup walnuts
2 tablespoons olive oil
14 ounces mixed oyster, chestnut,
and wild or field mushrooms,
  halved if large
salt and pepper
13 ounces dried egg tagliatelle
cep powder, to sprinkle (optional,
  see note)
chervil sprigs, to garnish

1 Soak the dried porcini in the wine for 30 minutes to soften. Strain the soaking liquid into a small heavy-based pan, squeezing out all excess liquid from the porcini.

2 Add the garlic to the pan, and simmer until softened and the liquid is reduced by half; take out the garlic and set aside. Stir the cream into the liquid; remove from the heat.

3 Chop the garlic, nuts, and porcini together, to a coarse paste. Heat the oil in a wok or pan, sauté and stir-fry the mushrooms over a high heat, adding firmer ones first. Season well. Lower the heat and stir in the walnut paste, then the sauce; heat through.

4 Add the tagliatelle to a large pan of boiling salted water and cook until al dente. Drain well and toss the pasta with the mushroom sauce. Serve dusted with cep powder, if wished, and scattered with chervil.

Note Cep powder adds a special finishing touch. It is available from larger supermarkets; or, to make your own, grind dried ceps to a powder in a coffee grinder.

Locate a good selection of mushrooms, including wild ones, if possible. Use mushroom-flavored tagliatelle if preferred.

Pasta with bacon and wilted spinach

1 pound dried spaghetti, tagliatelle,
  or linguine
salt and pepper
4 tablespoons olive oil
8 slices pancetta or unsmoked bacon,
  chopped

2 garlic cloves, minced
2 pounds spinach leaves, stalks
  removed
⅝ cup heavy cream
freshly grated nutmeg
3 tablespoons pine nuts, toasted

1 Bring a large pan of salted water to the boil. Add the pasta and cook until
al dente.
2 Meanwhile heat the oil in a large pan, add the pancetta or bacon, and fry
until just turning golden. Add the garlic and cook for 1 minute.
3 Stir in the spinach and cook over a high heat for a few minutes, or until
the leaves are just wilted. Pour in the cream, turning the spinach to ensure
it is well coated. Season with salt, pepper, and nutmeg. Heat until boiling.
4 Drain the pasta, keeping back 2 tablespoons water in the pan. Immediately
toss the pasta with the hot sauce. Serve sprinkled with the pine nuts.

Bacon, garlic, and spinach are mellowed
in a cream sauce. Don't overcook the fresh
spinach—it should be vivid green and full
of flavor.

Tuna tapenade

1¼ cup black olives (preferably Greek), stoned

2 tablespoons capers in brine, rinsed

10 canned anchovy fillets in oil, drained

¾ cup canned tuna fish in oil, drained

⅜ cup olive oil

1 canned red bell pepper, rinsed, seeded, and diced

2 tablespoons chopped fresh basil

lemon juice, to taste

salt and pepper

1 pound dried pasta shapes, such as ballerine, radiattore, casarecce, capelletti

1 Chop the olives, capers, anchovies, and tuna in a food processor.

2 With the motor running, add the oil in a steady stream, and mix briefly.

3 Transfer to a bowl, and stir in the diced pepper and chopped basil. Flavor with lemon juice, and season with salt and pepper to taste.

4 Bring a large pan of salted water to the boil. Add the pasta and cook until al dente. Drain, keeping 2 tablespoons water in the pan. Immediately toss the pasta with the sauce. Cover and leave to stand for 2–3 minutes before serving.

Tuna tapenade is an easy no-cook sauce for pasta. It relies on the heat of the cooked pasta to warm the ingredients.

Pasta with Mediterranean sauce

6 ounces soft fresh goat cheese

2 tablespoons capers in vinegar, drained

1⅛ cups mixed green and black olives, stoned and chopped

8 sun-dried tomatoes in oil, drained and chopped

1 teaspoon dried oregano (preferably freeze-dried)

salt and pepper

1 pound dried pasta shapes, such as ballerine, radiattore, casarecce, capelletti

1 In a bowl, mix the goat cheese with the capers, olives, sun-dried tomatoes, oregano, and seasoning to taste.

2 Cook the pasta in a large pan of salted water until al dente. Drain, keeping back 2 tablespoons water in the pan. Immediately toss the pasta with the sauce. Cover and let stand for 3 minutes before serving.

Sun-dried tomatoes, capers, olives, and goat cheese make a delicious no-cook sauce. The heat of the pasta melts the cheese to make a creamy sauce.

Rigatoni with cherry tomato and basil sauce

1 pound ripe cherry tomatoes,
   quartered
2 garlic cloves, finely chopped
4 tablespoons shredded fresh basil
⅝ cup extra-virgin olive oil
salt and pepper

1 pound dried chunky pasta shapes,
   such as rigatoni, penne, farfalle
¼ pound feta cheese, thinly sliced

1 In a bowl, mix the tomatoes with the garlic, basil, olive oil, and seasoning. Cover and leave to infuse for at least 30 minutes; do not refrigerate.
2 Bring a large pan of salted water to the boil. Add the pasta and cook until al dente. Drain, keeping back 2 tablespoons water in the pan. Immediately toss the pasta with the sauce. Cover with a lid and leave to stand for 3 minutes.
3 Remove the lid, stir, and serve topped with slices of feta.

A wonderfully fresh tasting pasta dish. Marinating the tomatoes with the garlic and basil is important to develop the flavors.

Pasta with garlic and anchovy sauce

3 tablespoons olive oil
3 garlic cloves, chopped
1 small can anchovies in oil, drained
  and chopped
15-ounce can chopped tomatoes
pepper

1 pound dried bucatini, macaroni, or
  other pasta shapes
10 large fresh basil leaves, shredded
¼ pound fresh arugula leaves

1 Heat the olive oil in a saucepan. Add the garlic and fry until just coloring. Stir in the anchovies and cook gently until they begin to dissolve.
2 Stir in the chopped tomatoes and bring to the boil. Season to taste with pepper (salt won't be needed, as the anchovies are quite salty). Cover and simmer gently for 10 minutes.
3 Meanwhile, bring a large pan of salted water to the boil. Add the pasta and cook until al dente. Drain the pasta, keeping back 2 tablespoons water in the pan.
4 Stir the shredded basil into the tomato and anchovy sauce. Immediately add to the pasta and toss well. Serve each portion topped with a tangle of arugula leaves.

Pasta in a classic tomato sauce infused with the savory saltiness of melted anchovies, topped with contrasting peppery arugula.

Finnan haddie frittata

Illustrated on previous pages

3 tablespoons butter
10 ounces skinless finnan haddie
   (smoked haddock) fillet
8 large eggs
4 tablespoons milk
salt and pepper
2 tablespoons minced green onion

2 tablespoons snipped chives
¾ cup cooked pasta twists or shells
   (i.e. ⅝ cup dried)
¼ pound sharp cheddar cheese,
   grated
snipped chives, to garnish

1 Heat half the butter in a large skillet. Add the smoked haddock, cover
tightly, and cook for 3 minutes. Lift out of the pan and flake roughly.
2 Beat the eggs with the milk, seasoning, green onion, chives, and cooked
pasta. Preheat the broiler.
3 Melt the remaining butter in the skillet, then pour in the egg mixture and
scatter half of the flaked fish over. Move the mixture round the pan with a
wooden spatula until half set.
4 Remove from the heat and top with the remaining smoked haddock.
Sprinkle with the cheese and extra chives. Broil for about 2 minutes until
set and puffy. Serve with a salad and crusty bread.

Note Make sure you use a cast-iron skillet or other type that is suitable for
placing under the broiler.

Variation Replace the smoked haddock with a 7 ounces of wafer-thin smoked
ham. Scrunch up the ham and scatter it over the frittata before sprinkling
with cheese.

Smoked haddock, mellow cheddar cheese
and a hint of onion give this omelet a
wonderful flavor, while the pasta makes it
a little more substantial.

Farfalle with shrimp

Serves 1

3 ounces dried farfalle or other pasta
 shapes
salt and pepper
3 ounces cooked shrimp
2 tabelspoons butter, softened
large pinch of cayenne pepper

freshly grated nutmeg (optional)
1 tablespoon finely chopped fresh
 parsley

1 Cook the pasta in a large pan of boiling salted water until al dente.
2 Drain the pasta, return to the pan and toss in the shrimp and butter.
Warm through until the butter melts.
3 Add the cayenne and grated nutmeg to taste, toss in the chopped parsley
and serve.

This simple dish is an ideal speedy supper
for one. Accompany with a tomato and
avocado salad, and warm bread.

Baked macaroni cheese with balsamic vinegar

1 cup dried elbow macaroni
salt and pepper
1¼ cup heavy cream
2 ounces gruyère cheese, grated
1 ounce Parmesan cheese, freshly
  grated
3 eggs, beaten

For the dressing
1 shallot, minced
2 ripe tomatoes, peeled, seeded and
  diced
6 tablespoons extra-virgin olive oil
few fresh thyme leaves
1 tablespoon balsamic vinegar

1 Preheat oven to 350°F. Oil and line the base of 4 timbales or ovenproof cups.
2 Cook the pasta in boiling salted water until al dente. Drain thoroughly
and divide between the timbales or cups.
3 Slowly bring the cream to the boil in a pan. Remove from the heat, season,
and stir in the cheeses until melted. Stir into the beaten eggs. Pour the
savory custard over the macaroni.
4 Stand the molds in a roasting pan, half filled with boiling water. Bake
for 25 minutes.
5 Remove the molds from the pan of water; let rest for 5 minutes. Warm
the dressing ingredients together in a small pan for 5 minutes or until the
shallots are softened; season with salt and pepper to taste.
6 Turn out the pasta molds onto warmed plates, and surround with the
tomato dressing. Garnish with thyme to serve.

Macaroni baked in a savory cheese custard
in timbales, then turned out and served with
a piquant tomato sauce.

easy
fish

Peppered salmon with juniper and vermouth

1 teaspoon dried green peppercorns
16 juniper berries
1 teaspoon salt
4 salmon steaks or fillets, skinned
2 tablespoons unsalted butter

8 tablespoons dry vermouth
(preferably Noilly Prat)
2–3 tablespoons heavy cream or
crème fraîche

1 Crush together the peppercorns, juniper berries, and salt, using a pestle and mortar (or end of a rolling pin and strong bowl). Sprinkle over the salmon and press well to adhere.

2 Melt the butter in a skillet over a medium heat, and fry the seasoned fish for about 10–12 minutes for steaks, a little less for salmon fillets, turning once.

3 Lift the salmon onto a warm serving dish; keep warm while you finish the sauce.

4 Deglaze the pan with the vermouth and let bubble for 2–3 minutes until syrupy. Stir in the cream or crème fraîche and let bubble for 2 minutes. Spoon the sauce over the salmon to serve.

Note If buying salmon by the piece to cut into portions, choose the middle or tail end, as this is less oily than the head end.

An easy dish with intriguing flavors—
delicious with herbed mashed potatoes.

Basque baked fish in parchment

Illustrated on previous pages

4 cod or haddock fillets, each
  6–7 ounces, skinned
½ green bell pepper, cored, seeded,
  and diced
½ red bell pepper, cored, seeded, and
  diced
1 onion, finely chopped
1 tablespoon fresh oregano leaves,
  chopped

2 garlic cloves, finely chopped
2 plum tomatoes, skinned, seeded,
  and chopped
juice of 1 lemon
1 tablespoon olive oil
4 tablespoons dry white wine
salt and pepper
12 black olives (optional)

1 Preheat oven to 375°F. Cut 4 sheets of nonstick baking parchment, measuring approximately 12 x15inches. Place each fish fillet on a piece of paper, positioning it slightly off center.

2 In a bowl, mix together the peppers, onion, oregano, garlic, tomatoes, lemon juice, olive oil, and wine. Season with salt and pepper.

3 Spoon the mixture on top of the fish, and scatter the olives over, if using. Fold the parchment over the fish to form a triangle. Fold the edges together tightly to form a sealed parcel.

4 Lift the parcels onto a baking sheet, and bake for 15–20 minutes until the fish is cooked through. Place each parcel on a warmed plate, and serve at once, with buttery new potatoes and steamed broccoli.

These fish parcels cook quickly and easily in the oven, trapping in the flavors of sweet peppers, onion, garlic, and oregano.

Portuguese baked fish and potato

1 pound 10 ounces thick cod fillets, skinned
5 tablespoons olive oil
3 large onions, halved and thinly sliced
3 garlic cloves, finely chopped
1 pound 5 ounces baking potatoes
3 tablespoons finely chopped fresh parsley
16 black olives, stoned and roughly chopped
salt and pepper
⅝ cup fish or chicken stock
For the garnish
4 hard-boiled eggs, quartered
chopped flat leaf parsley

1 Preheat oven to 350°F. Place the fish fillets on a lightly oiled baking sheet, brush with olive oil, and bake for 7–10 minutes. Let cool slightly.
2 Meanwhile, heat the remaining oil in a large skillet, add the onions, and sauté for about 20 minutes until golden brown. Add the garlic and sauté for 2 minutes; set aside.
3 In the meantime, boil the potatoes until tender. Drain and leave to cool slightly, then peel and cut into ½-inch slices.
4 When the fish is cool enough to handle, separate into large flakes.
5 Lightly oil a shallow ovenproof dish, 9¼–10inches in diameter. Layer the potatoes, onions, parsley, olives, and fish in the dish, seasoning each layer generously and finishing with a layer of onions. Pour in the stock, and bake for 20 minutes.
6 Serve garnished with hard-boiled eggs and chopped parsley. Accompany with green beans or roasted tomatoes.

Flavored with caramelized onions, black olives, and garlic, this tasty dish is best enjoyed with a glass of rioja.

Warm smoked cod and butter bean salad

4 small cooked beets, diced
2 teaspoons cider vinegar
1 pound 2 ounces undyed smoked
  cod fillet, skinned
1 bunch watercress, trimmed

15-ounce can butter beans, drained
3 green onions, finely sliced
pepper

1 Toss the diced beets in the cider vinegar; set aside.
2 Poach the haddock in just enough water to cover for 4–5 minutes
until opaque; drain.
3 Meanwhile gently mix the watercress sprigs, butter beans, onions, and
beets together in a shallow serving bowl.
4 When the fish is cool enough to handle, divide into flakes, and scatter
over the salad. Season with plenty of pepper.

Note The beets lightly tinge the beans a pretty pale pink. Combine the salad
shortly before serving to avoid over-coloring.

Smoky cod marries with sweet beets and
creamy butter beans to make a substantial
but low-fat meal.

Tagliatelle, smoked salmon and pesto

Illustrated on previous pages

1 cup blanched whole almonds
1 garlic clove, finely chopped
2 tablespoons freshly grated
  Parmesan cheese
3 handfuls fresh parsley leaves,
  roughly chopped
⅝ cup light olive oil

3 tablespoons crème fraîche
salt and pepper
1 pound 2 ounces dried tagliatelle
½ pound sliced smoked salmon, cut
  into strips
flat leaf parsley, to garnish

1 Spread the almonds on a baking sheet and place under the broiler for
1–2 minutes, turning frequently, until toasted and golden. Allow to cool,
then chop roughly. Beat together with the garlic, Parmesan, parsley, olive
oil, and crème fraîche. Season with salt and pepper to taste.
2 Add the tagliatelle to a large pan of boiling salted water, and cook
according to the packet directions until al dente (cooked, but still firm
to the bite). Drain, keeping back 2–3 tablespoons of the cooking water.
3 Add the parsley pesto to the pasta, and toss well to mix. Pile into warmed
bowls, and top each serving with a tangle of smoked salmon. Garnish with
flat leaf parsley, and serve at once.

Note Don't be tempted to puree the pesto ingredients in a food processor
until smooth. A coarse-textured pesto gives a better result for this recipe.

Tagliatelle is tossed with a coarse pesto of
toasted almonds, garlic, parsley, Parmesan, and
olive oil, then topped with smoked salmon.

Baked salmon and potatoes

1½ pounds potatoes, skin on, thinly
  sliced
6 tablespoons butter, melted
1 teaspoon celery or fennel seeds
salt and pepper

1½ pounds skinless salmon fillet (tail
  end)
3 tablespoons light cream
chopped flat leaf parsley, to garnish

1 Preheat oven to 400°F. Parboil the potatoes in water or stock for
4–5 minutes; the slices must remain whole. Drain and refresh under cold
water; drain.
2 Line a buttered shallow 7x10-inch ovenproof dish with half of the
potatoes, brushing with butter and sprinkling with celery or fennel seed,
salt, and pepper.
3 Cut the fish into chunks and lay over the potato; season and drizzle the
cream over. Top with the remaining potato, seasoning as before. Bake for
40 minutes until the topping is crisp. Garnish with parsley.

Salmon fillet is baked between layers of potato
and celery seed, keeping it moist, while the
potato topping becomes crisp.

Crab and papaya salad

Illustrated on previous pages

¾ pound fresh white crab meat
(see note)

2 ripe tomatoes, skinned, seeded,
and diced

1 red chili, seeded and finely
chopped

2 tablespoons chopped fresh cilantro
leaves

2 tablespoons extra-virgin olive oil

3 tablespoons lime juice

few drops of Tabasco sauce

1 small papaya

salt and pepper

2 trevise or Belgian endive bulbs

a little extra-virgin olive oil

squeeze of lime juice

cilantro leaves and lime wedges,
to garnish

1 Carefully pick over the crabmeat discarding any small pieces of shell
or cartilage, then place in a bowl.

2 Stir in the tomatoes, chili, cilantro, olive oil, lime juice, and Tabasco sauce.
Cover and leave to infuse in the refrigerator for at least 1 hour.

3 Just before serving, peel the papaya and scoop out the seeds. Dice the
papaya flesh and stir into the crabmeat. Check the seasoning.

4 Separate the trevise or endive leaves and dress with a little olive oil and
lime juice. Arrange on individual serving plates. Spoon the crab salad on top
and garnish with cilantro leaves. Serve immediately, with lime wedges and
warm French bread.

Note If you prefer to buy a whole crab, choose one that weighs at least
3 pounds to obtain the required amount of white meat.

Either buy a freshly dressed crab or use
vacuum-packed fresh crabmeat for this tangy
crab salad.

Potted crab with ginger and garlic

4 small dressed crabs, each about
  6 ounces
1 stick (8 tablespoons) unsalted
  butter
¾-inch piece fresh gingerroot, peeled
  and grated

1 garlic clove, crushed
1 teaspoon sweet paprika
salt and pepper

1 Scoop the meat out of the crab shells.
2 Melt the butter slowly in a small saucepan. Add the ginger and garlic, and cook over a gentle heat for 3–5 minutes until soft but not colored.
3 Add the paprika and crab. Stir to coat with the butter and heat through; season with salt and pepper to taste.
4 Spoon the crab mixture into ramekins, and smooth the tops. Allow to cool, then chill in the refrigerator for at least 1 hour to set.
5 Serve the potted crab with warm toasted pita bread fingers.

Note Small ready-prepared fresh crabs are obtainable from some supermarket fresh fish counters.

Fresh, ready-prepared crab, mixed with a spiced clarified butter and set in ramekins. Serve with warm, toasted pita bread.

Smoked mackerel and spinach frittata

Illustrated on previous pages

Serves 3–4

1 pound ready-prepared young,
fresh spinach
2 tablespoons olive oil
½ pound smoked mackerel fillets
6 ounces small new potatoes
salt and pepper
1 stick (8 tablespoons) butter
6 large eggs
2 ounces Parmesan cheese, freshly
grated

1 Remove any tough stems from the spinach. Heat the oil in a skillet, add
the spinach, and toss until just wilted; transfer to a plate. Remove the skin
from the mackerel fillets and roughly flake the flesh.
2 Cook the potatoes in boiling salted water for 15–20 minutes until just
tender. Drain and allow to cool slightly, then slice thickly.
3 Heat half the butter in a nonstick skillet, and sauté the potatoes for
5 minutes or until beginning to color.
4 In a bowl, beat the eggs with half of the Parmesan, a good pinch of salt,
and plenty of pepper. Stir in the spinach and potatoes.
5 Melt the remaining butter in a 10-inch heavy, nonstick skillet. When
foaming, pour in the egg mixture. Turn down the heat as low as possible.
Cook for about 15 minutes until set, with the top still a little runny. Scatter
the flaked mackerel over and sprinkle with the remaining Parmesan.
6 Place briefly under a hot broiler to lightly brown the cheese and just set
the top; do not over-brown, or the frittata will dry out. Slide onto a warm
plate and cut into wedges. Serve with a crisp salad.

This Italian omelet is cooked slowly, and the
filling is stirred into the eggs or scattered on
top. A frittata is served just set, never folded.

Pan-fried monkfish or cod with mustard

3 tablespoons unsalted butter
2 monkfish or cod fillets, each about
   10 ounces, skinned and thickly
   sliced
1 garlic clove, crushed

½ cup extra-dry white vermouth
1 tablespoon Dijon mustard
⅝ cup heavy cream
1 tablespoon snipped fresh chives
   (optional)

1 Melt the butter in a large skillet, and briefly fry the fish for 1–2 minutes until almost cooked. Lift from the pan.
2 Add the garlic to the pan, and fry gently until softened. Add the vermouth and mustard, and bubble vigorously to boil off the alcohol.
3 Stir in the cream, and chives, if using, then return the fish to the pan to warm through and finish cooking. Serve with tagliatelle and sugar-snap peas or snow peas.

Flash-fried monkfish slices in a creamy mustard sauce, with a dash of vermouth.

Herring with mustard lemon butter

1 cup pinhead oatmeal or dry white
   breadcrumbs
grated rind and juice of 1 lemon
4 large herring fillets
½ cup milk
4 tablespoons butter

1 lemon, thinly sliced
1 tablespoon wholegrain mustard
2 tablespoons chopped fresh parsley
salt and pepper

1 Mix the oatmeal with the lemon rind. Dip the fish into the milk, then into the oatmeal to coat on both sides.
2 Melt the butter in a large skillet, and fry the fish with the lemon slices for about 2 minutes on each side; transfer to warm plates, and keep warm.
3 Add the lemon juice, mustard, and parsley to the pan, and heat until bubbling; season. Pour over the herring and serve.

Fillets of herring are dipped in oatmeal mixed with grated lemon rind, then pan-fried in butter flavored with lemon and parsley.

Salmon baguette

Serves 2

1 baguette, about 2 inches
   across, 8–9 inches in length,
4–6 tablespoons pesto
9 ounces fresh salmon fillet
pepper

1 Preheat oven to 425°F. Split a baguette, without cutting right through.
Spread both cut faces with pesto.
2 Finely slice the fresh salmon fillet into ¼-inch slices. Fill the baguette with
the salmon, overlapping the slices, and season with pepper.
3 Wrap the baguette in oiled foil, and bake for about 30 minutes. Open the
foil slightly to let out steam, and then return to the oven for a few minutes.
Cut the baguette in half, and serve in napkins.

An original meal for two. Simply split a
baguette, spread with herb butter, sandwich
with thin slices of salmon fillet, then bake.

Pan-seared gravlax on mashed celeriac

½ pound celeriac
½ pound potatoes
salt and pepper
⅝ cup milk
2 tablespoons olive oil
1–2 tablespoons sweet dill mustard

2 large dill pickles, chopped
8 green onions, finely sliced
2 tablespoons butter
1 pound sliced gravlax

1 Peel the celeriac and potatoes, and cut into even-sized pieces. Add to a pan of cold salted water, bring to the boil, and cook for 15–20 minutes until tender. Drain thoroughly, then mash well.
2 Heat the milk with the olive oil, mustard, dill pickles, and green onions. Beat into the mashed celeriac and potatoes: keep warm.
3 Heat the butter in a heavy-based skillet until sizzling. Fry the gravlax, in two batches, over a high heat until just starting to color.
4 Pile the mashed celeriac and potatoes onto warmed serving plates, and top with the gravlax. Pour on any pan juices and serve immediately.

Thin slices of gravlax are quickly fried in butter and served on a pile of mashed celeriac and potatoes, flavored with dill mustard, chopped dill pickles, and green onions.

Trout with dill pickle and capers

Serves 2

2 whole trout, cleaned

2 tablespoons seasoned flour

2 tablespoons unsalted butter

juice of ½ small lemon

½ large dill pickle, finely chopped

1–2 teaspoons capers

1–2 tablespoons flat leaf parsley,
  roughly chopped

salt and pepper

1 Coat the trout in seasoned flour. Melt the butter in a large skillet, then fry the trout for 5 minutes each side or until cooked and the skin is crisp. Lift onto warm plates.

2 Pour the lemon juice into the pan juices. Warm through with the pickle, capers, and parsley. Season to taste, then pour over the trout. Serve with a salad and potatoes.

Pan-fried trout with a piquant sauce of lemon butter, capers, dill pickle, and parsley.

Spicy broiled sardines

4 garlic cloves, crushed
½ teaspoon hot paprika
1 teaspoon ground cumin
1 tablespoon lemon juice
1 tablespoon olive oil
salt and pepper
12–16 fresh sardines, depending
  on size, cleaned

For the salad
5 oranges
1 red onion, very thinly sliced
2 small handfuls flat leaf parsley
  leaves, roughly torn
16 large black olives (optional)
extra-virgin olive oil, for drizzling

1 Mix the garlic with the spices, lemon juice, olive oil, and seasoning.
Rub this mixture all over the sardines to coat thoroughly. Set aside.
2 For the salad, peel and segment the oranges, discarding all white pith,
membrane, and seeds. Place the orange segments in a bowl with the red
onion, chopped parsley, and black olives, if using. Season with salt and
pepper to taste, and drizzle with a little olive oil.
3 Preheat the broiler. Place the sardines on the rack in the broiler pan, and
broil for approximately 2 minutes each side until cooked through. Serve
with the orange salad and warm crusty bread.

Note Before broiling the sardines, add a little water to the broiler pan.
This will prevent any juices from the fish from burning on the pan base,
which causes smoking.

Fresh sardines are available from many fish
markets. Here they are broiled with a spicy
garlic coating and served with a refreshing
Moroccan orange salad.

Mussels steamed in a paper bag

Illustrated on previous pages

3¼ pounds fresh mussels in shells
2 tablespoons olive oil
1 garlic clove, chopped
2 celery sticks, cut into fine julienne strips
1 red bell pepper, cored, seeded, and finely sliced

1 red chile, seeded and finely diced
1 teaspoon Szechuan peppercorns, crushed
4 tablespoons teriyaki marinade

1 To clean the mussels, if necessary, scrub in several changes of water, discarding any that do not close when sharply tapped. Pull off any "beards" that are still attached.

2 Preheat oven to 450°F. Heat the oil in a skilletn and add the garlic, celery, red pepper, and chile. Stir-fry over a brisk heat for 1 minute. Add the crushed peppercorns and take off the heat.

3 Cut four 12-inch squares of baking parchment. Divide the mussels between the paper squares, piling them in the center. Top with the stir-fried vegetables, and pour 1 tablespoon teriyaki marinade over each portion. Bring the sides of the paper up over the mussels to enclose them like a bag; tie with cotton string. Place on a baking tray.

4 Place in the oven for 10 minutes or until the mussels open (squeeze bags to check). Serve immediately, in the paper bags!

Note Make sure guests discard any mussels that have not opened.

Mussels are quick and easy, especially if you buy ready-cleaned ones and cook them in this unusual way.

Salt-baked hake

Serves 2.
1 hake, about 1¼ pound, cleaned
1 tablespoon Maldon sea salt flakes
few fresh rosemary branches
lemon wedges, to serve

1 Preheat oven to 425°F. Snip the fins off the fish, using kitchen scissors. Wash fish under running cold water. Shake off excess moisture, then, holding on to the tail, toss the fish in the salt so that it all adheres.
2 Lay the rosemary over the base of an ovenproof dish, and place the fish on top. Immediately bake for about 20 minutes until cooked through.
3 To serve, break away and discard the salted fish skin. Serve the fish accompanied by lemon wedges, warm bread, and a tomato, olive, and red onion salad.

Hake is an inexpensive white fish with a fine flavor. Here it is encrusted in salt just before baking, to seal in the flavor and juices. The flesh stays moist and, perhaps surprisingly, it isn't too salty.

Flounder, anchovies and Parmesan

Illustrated on previous pages

8 flounder fillets, skinned
4 anchovy fillets, finely chopped
1 cup heavy cream
5 tablespoons fresh brown
   breadcrumbs
2 tablespoons finely chopped parsley

8 tablespoons finely grated fresh
   Parmesan cheese

1 Heat oven to 400°F. Halve each fillet lengthwise along the natural line. Dot with the anchovies.
2 Roll up each fillet from the thicker end. Arrange the fish, spiral side uppermost, in 4 individual gratin dishes and spoon the cream over.
3 Mix the breadcrumbs with the parsley and Parmesan, and scatter over the flounder. Bake for 8–10 minutes until the fish is cooked and the topping is golden. Serve with a salad, or broiled tomatoes and baby potatoes.

Plaice fillets are rolled around chopped anchovies, then dotted with cream, and baked under a cheese and herb crumb topping.

Cod with creamy white bean stew

2 tablespoons olive oil
2 garlic cloves, finely chopped
2 tablespoons finely shredded fresh
   sage
1 red chile, seeded and finely
   chopped

15-ounce can cannellini beans,
   drained
⅝ cup fish or vegetable stock
4 tablespoons butter
2 onions, halved and thinly sliced
4 cod steaks, each about 6 ounces

1 Heat half the oil in a pan; fry the garlic until golden. Add the sage and chile; cook for 1 minute. Add the beans and stock, bring to the boil and simmer for 20 minutes; season.
2 Meanwhile, melt the butter in a small pan. Stir in the onions, add 2 tablespoons water and cover tightly. Simmer gently for 20–25 minutes until very soft, stirring occasionally.
3 Brush the cod steaks with oil, season, and broil for 2–3 minutes on each side. Serve on the bean stew, topped with the onions.

Grilled cod steaks served on meltingly soft cannellini beans, flavored with chile, garlic, and sage, and topped with caramelized onions.

Steamed sea bass with fennel

Serves 2.

1 tablespoon olive oil

3 small fennel bulbs, trimmed, each
    cut into 8 wedges, feathery fronds
    reserved

½ teaspoon cardamom seeds (from
    3–4 pods)

2¼ cups vegetable stock

1 sea bass, about 1 pounds
    10 ounces, cleaned

salt and pepper

1 Heat the oil in a wide, heavy-based deep pot or flameproof casserole,
add the fennel with the cardamom seeds, and fry until lightly browned
and slightly softened.

2 Add the stock and bring to the boil. Lower the heat, cover, and simmer
for 10 minutes.

3 Season the fish and place on its side on top of the fennel. Cover tightly
and cook over a medium heat for 15–20 minutes. To make sure the fish is
cooked, insert a knife in the thickest part of the back and check that the
flesh is opaque.

4 Carefully lift the fish onto a serving dish, and surround with the fennel
wedges. Spoon the pan juices over the fish, and garnish with the reserved
fennel fronds. Serve with warm crusty bread or plain boiled potatoes to mop
up the juices.

Note Most white fish have low-fat flesh because their oil is stored in the liver.
Oily fish, such as sardines, salmon, tuna, and trout, have oil distributed
throughout their flesh and are therefore relatively high in fat but full of
beneficial fish oils and vitamins.

The delicate flavors in this fragrant one-pot
meal are retained during cooking.

easy
chicken

Chicken with pawpaw and rice noodles

½ pound skinless chicken breast
fillets

¼ pound rice vermicelli noodles

1 small carrot, cut into julienne
strips

1 small pawpaw, peeled, seeded, and
diced

2 tablespoons fresh cilantro leaves,
roughly torn

For the marinade

1 tablespoon Thai fish sauce

1 teaspoon sesame oil

1 teaspoon Thai red curry paste

1 teaspoon clear honey

For the dressing

3 tablespoons sunflower oil

1 tablespoon superfine sugar

3 tablespoons lime juice

1½ tablespoon Thai fish sauce or soy
sauce

1 red chili, seeded and chopped

1 First mix the marinade ingredients in a dish. Cut the chicken into strips, toss in the marinade, and leave for 1 hour.

2 Soak the noodles in boiling water for 4–5 minutes or according to pack instructions. Drain, dry well, and place in a large bowl. Add the carrot, pawpaw, and cilantro.

3 Mix the dressing ingredients together, toss half with the noodles, and chill until required.

4 Heat a wok or large skillet until smoking. Add the chicken with the marinade, and stir-fry over a high heat until cooked through. Divide the chicken and noodles between 4 bowls, and serve drizzled with the remaining dressing.

This warm salad of hot, spicy chicken tossed with cool pawpaw, carrot, and rice noodles epitomizes the fresh tastes of Thai food.

Goujons with avocado mayonnaise

4 slices day-old white bread
2 teaspoons poppy seeds
¼ teaspoon cayenne pepper
2 tablespoons snipped fresh chives
4 skinless chicken breast fillets,
 thickly sliced
2 eggs, beaten
4 tablespoons sunflower oil, for
 frying

For the mayonnaise
1 large avocado, halved and stoned
3 tablespoons mayonnaise
2 tablespoons vinaigrette dressing
salt and pepper

1 First blend the mayonnaise ingredients together in a food processor until creamy; turn into a bowl. Clean the processor.
2 Break the bread into the food processor. Add the spices, chives, and 1 teaspoon salt. Process to crumbs; tip onto a plate. Dip the chicken strips in the egg, then into the spicy crumbs to coat.
3 Heat the oil in a large nonstick skillet, and fry the goujons for 2–3 minutes each side until crisp and golden. Serve hot, with the avocado mayonnaise and a salad.

Poppy seeds, chives, and cayenne add a savory note to these crunchy chicken strips. An avocado dip is the perfect foil.

Seared chicken with marsala and sage

Serves 6

4 free-range chicken breast fillets,
   skinned
salt and pepper
2 tablespoons sunflower oil
12 fresh sage leaves

6 tablespoons butter
1 tablespoon chopped fresh sage
¾ cup marsala

1 Cut each chicken fillet lengthwise into 6 strips and season lightly. Heat the oil in a skillet and fry the sage leaves, a few at a time, for a few seconds; lift out and drain on paper towels.

2 Melt some of the butter in a heavy-based pan, and sear the chicken in batches over a high heat to brown all over. Return all chicken to the pan; add the chopped sage.

3 Pour in a little marsala. As it reduces to a syrup, continue to add marsala, a little at a time, until only about 2 tablespoons remain. Lift the chicken onto warmed plates.

4 Deglaze the pan with the remaining marsala, and pour over the chicken. Top with the fried sage leaves to serve.

This is quick enough to cook between courses. Serve on a large bread croûte with colorful salad leaves.

Rosemary and lemon chicken with olives

Serves 6

12 skinless, boneless chicken thighs

1 unwaxed lemon, halved

6 tablespoons olive oil

6 garlic cloves, peeled and halved
lengthwise

2 onions, halved and sliced

10 fresh rosemary sprigs

2 pounds potatoes (preferably
organic), peeled

1 teaspoon ground black pepper

2 teaspoons Malden sea salt flakes

18 kalamata olives

1 Trim the chicken thighs of any excess fat and cut them in half. Place in
a bowl, squeeze the lemon juice over the meat, and toss well; leave to stand
for 10 minutes. Discard one of the lemon shells; cut the other into slivers,
and set aside.

2 Preheat oven to 425°F. Drain the chicken and pat each piece dry. Place in
a large shallow roasting pan in a single layer. Mix in the lemon slivers, olive
oil, garlic, onions, and 5 rosemary sprigs; leave to stand for 20 minutes.

3 Cut the potatoes into 1½-inch pieces. Add to a pan of boiling water, bring
back to the boil, and parboil for 2 minutes only; drain well.

4 Add the potatoes to the chicken, and sprinkle with the pepper and half of
the salt. Bake in the oven for 50 minutes, turning all the ingredients every
10 minutes. If there is a lot of liquid from the onions 10 minutes before the
end, increase the heat to 475°F.

5 About 5 minutes before the end of the cooking time, replace the rosemary
with fresh sprigs, and add the olives. Serve sprinkled with the remaining
salt flakes.

As the flavors of this effortless all-in-one meal
are robust, serve with a well dressed salad.

Lemon chciken with garlic and potatoes

Illustrated on previous pages

8–12 chicken pieces (thighs and
    drumsticks)
salt and pepper
finely grated rind of 1 lemon
2 tablespoons chopped fresh thyme
2 pounds small new potatoes

1 lemon, very thinly sliced
12 large garlic cloves (unpeeled)
⅝ cup olive oil

1 Preheat oven to 350°F. Put the chicken in a large bowl, season well, and add the lemon rind and thyme. Toss well to coat, and spread in a large baking dish.

2 Crack each potato by tapping sharply with a rolling pin. Add to the chicken. Tuck the lemon slices around. Scatter the garlic cloves over the chicken. Drizzle the olive oil evenly over the top.

3 Bake for about 45 minutes, stirring occasionally, until golden brown and cooked through. Serve with zucchini or broccoli.

Try this as an alternative to the traditional Sunday roast—it's all done in one dish!

Chicken with pancetta and asparagus

Serves 6

6 ounces asparagus tips

6 free-range chicken breast fillets, skinned

salt and pepper

18 slices pancetta

2 tablespoons olive oil

chervil or parsley sprigs, to garnish

1 Cook the asparagus in boiling water for 2 minutes, then drain and refresh in cold water; drain again and pat dry with paper towels.

2 Slice horizontally into each chicken breast without cutting all the way through, then open out. Place, two at a time, between sheets of waxed paper, and beat with a rolling pin to flatten out slightly.

3 Preheat oven to 375°F. Season each chicken breast lightly, and cover with 1½ slices of pancetta. Place 4 asparagus tips lengthwise on top, and roll up. Brush the chicken parcels with a little oil, and wrap each one in another 1½ slices of pancetta.

4 Wrap each parcel tightly in foil to seal and hold in the juices. Place on a baking sheet, and bake in the oven for 20 minutes.

5 Leave to rest in a warm place for 5–15 minutes, then remove the foil. Slice the chicken parcels into rounds, and serve on a bed of rice, with any juices poured over. Garnish with chervil or parsley.

NOTE Packets of thinly sliced pancetta are available from larger supermarkets. Alternatively, you can buy pancetta freshly sliced from Italian delicatessens.

These are very easy to prepare, hours in advance. Serve sliced to reveal the pretty asparagus and pancetta.

Chicken potpies with mashed butternut

1 pound 2 ounces butternut squash, peeled, seeded, and diced
2¼ pounds potatoes, peeled and diced
1¼ cup milk
1 teaspoon chopped fresh sage
2 tablespoons butter
4 skinless chicken breast fillets, cut into 1-inch cubes
salt and pepper

1 small cooking apple, peeled, cored, and chopped
2 leeks, sliced
⅝ cup dry hard cider
1 chicken stock cube
2 ounces sharp cheddar cheese, grated

1 Put the butternut squash, potatoes, milk, chopped sage, and butter in a pan, and season with salt and pepper. Bring to the boil, lower the heat, cover the pan tightly, and simmer for 20–25 minutes, stirring once, until the potatoes are tender. Mash until the mixture is smooth.

2 Meanwhile, put the chicken in a pan with the apple, leeks, cider, and stock. Season, cover, and simmer gently for 25 minutes until the leeks and chicken are tender and the apple is pulpy.

3 Spoon the chicken mixture over the base of four 12-ounce (approx. 5-inch diameter) potpie dishes and top with the mashed potatoes and squash. Sprinkle with the cheese. If preparing ahead, cover and keep chilled for up to 2 days.

4 To serve, preheat oven to 375°F. Bake the pies for 30 minutes until golden and piping hot. Serve with broccoli or cabbage.

Tasty pies filled with chicken, leeks, and tart apple cooked in cider. Butternut squash gives a sweet flavor to the mashed potato topping.

Skewered rosemary chicken

4 skinless chicken breast fillets, cut
   into 1-inch cubes
1 clove garlic, crushed
2 teaspoons chopped fresh thyme
juice of ½ lemon
salt and pepper

8 fresh rosemary stems, at least
   9 inches long (preferably woody)

1 Put the chicken in a non-metallic bowl, and add the garlic, thyme, lemon juice, and seasoning. Toss well and leave to marinate for 30–40 minutes (no longer), turning occasionally.
2 Strip the rosemary stems of their leaves, except for the 3 inches at the narrow end. Cut the woody ends obliquely to shape points that will pierce the chicken.
3 Preheat the broiler. Remove the chicken from the marinade, reserving the juice.
4 Thread the chicken pieces onto the skewers carefully; lay on the grill tray, with the leafy rosemary tips toward you.
5 Cover the rosemary leaves with a strip of foil to prevent them from scorching. Broil for about 10–15 minutes, turning and basting occasionally with the reserved marinade.Serve with a mixed salad.

Grilling meat on herb skewers gives off a wonderful aroma to stimulate the tastebuds.

Lime and ginger broiled chicken

4 skinless chicken breast fillets
½ teaspoon finely grated lime rind
juice of ½ large lime
1-inch piece fresh gingerroot, finely
  shredded
salt and pepper

2 teaspoons maple syrup or clear
  honey
snipped chives, to garnish

1 Using a very sharp knife, score the chicken deeply in a crisscross pattern, cutting halfway through the thickness. Place in a shallow dish.
2 Mix together the lime rind and juice, ginger, and seasoning. Brush this over the scored surface of the chicken, and leave to marinate for about 20 minutes.
3 Preheat the broiler to high. Brush the chicken with the maple syrup or honey and cook for 7–8 minutes on each side, turning and basting at least twice.
4 Serve garnished with snipped chives and accompanied by steamed green beans or sugar-snap peas.

Lean chicken breast fillets are deeply scored before marinating to encourage the flavors to permeate and ensure quick cooking.

Rancher's chicken

Serves 2

2 skinless chicken breast fillets
1 large tomato, finely chopped
2 tablespoon hickory barbecue sauce
1 tablespoon olive oil

4 strips rindless smoked bacon
2 ounces sharp cheddar cheese,
 grated

1 Beat the chicken fillets with a rolling pin until flattened to an even thickness. Stir the tomato into the hickory sauce.
2 Heat the oil in a large cast-iron (or other ovenproof) skillet, add the chicken, and bacon, and fry for about 1–2 minutes each side. Preheat the broiler.
3 Space the chicken fillets apart in the pan, then spread with the tomato mixture. Sprinkle with the cheese and top with the bacon.
4 Broil for about 3 minutes until the bacon is turning golden and the cheese has melted. Serve with a salad and baked potatoes.

This takes minutes to make, yet the smoky sauce adds a special taste.

Chicken with lemon and minted couscous

Illustrated on previous pages

finely grated rind and juice of
2 lemons
2 garlic cloves, crushed
2 teaspoons ground cumin
8–12 chicken pieces (thighs and
drumsticks)
4 tablespoons olive oil
salt and pepper

8 green onions, sliced
1½ cups chicken stock
(approximately)
6 tablespoons chopped fresh mint
1¼ cups quick-cook couscous
lemon wedges and mint sprigs,
to garnish

1 Preheat oven to 400°F. Mix the juice and rind of 1 lemon with the garlic and cumin. Rub this mixture all over the chicken pieces.
2 Spoon 2 tablespoons of the olive oil over the base of a baking dish and add the chicken. Season, then add ⅝ cup water. Bake in the oven for 25–30 minutes.
3 Meanwhile, heat the remaining olive oil in a pan, add the green onions, and fry gently for 2–3 minutes until starting to color. Stir in the remaining lemon rind and juice. Pour in the stock and bring to the boil.
4 Add the mint, then pour in the couscous in a steady stream, stirring briefly to mix. Cover, remove from the heat, and leave to swell for 10 minutes. Fork through the grains to break up any lumps; re-cover, and keep warm.
5 Transfer the couscous and chicken to warmed plates. If necessary, deglaze the baking dish with a little extra stock or water, and drizzle the pan juices over the chicken and couscous. Serve garnished with lemon wedges and mint sprigs.

Simple baked chicken served on a bed of lemon couscous flavored with mint.

Tagliatelle with lime chicken

Serves 3–4

2 large skinless chicken breast fillets

2 teaspoons sesame oil

1 tablespoon dark soy sauce

½ teaspoon chile sauce

10 ounces dried tagliatelle

4 green onions, thickly sliced

For the sauce

1¼ cup chicken or vegetable stock
(see note)

generous ¾ cup coconut cream

1½ teaspoon Thai fish sauce

6 kaffir lime leaves, shredded

1 garlic clove, sliced

pinch of sugar

salt and pepper

For the garnish

cilantro leaves

1 Cut the chicken into strips and toss with the sesame oil, soy sauce, and chile sauce. Cover and leave to marinate in a cool place for 1 hour.

2 Meanwhile, prepare the sauce. Place all the ingredients in a saucepan, bring to the boil, and simmer until reduced by half. Pass through a fine sieve and keep warm.

3 Bring a large pan of salted water to the boil. Add the pasta and cook until al dente.

4 Meanwhile, heat a wok or large skillet until hot. Add the chicken and stir-fry for 4–5 minutes until browned and cooked thorough. Add the green onions, toss well, and remove from the heat.

5 Drain the pasta and spoon into warmed bowls. Top with the chicken and green onion mixture and drizzle the lime sauce over. Serve at once, garnished with cilantro leaves.

NOTE For the sauce use homemade or bought fresh stock, which is available from some supermarkets' chilled cabinets.

This combination of chile chicken, noodles and a creamy lime sauce is a wonderful fusion of flavors.

Japanese chicken skewers

4 tablespoons Japanese soy sauce

2 tablespoons saké or medium-dry sherry

1 tablespoon superfine sugar

8 boneless chicken thighs, skinned

For the cucumber salad

1 small cucumber

½ teaspoon salt

scant 1 cup arame or hijiki seaweed (optional)

1-inch piece fresh gingerroot, peeled

2 tablespoons rice wine vinegar

1 tablespoon superfine sugar

1 Put the soy sauce, saké or sherry, and sugar in a small pan and heat gently until the sugar is dissolved. Set aside to cool.

2 Cut the chicken into bite-size cubes, place in a dish, add the soy mix, and marinate for 2 hours. Soak 4 bamboo skewers in cold water for 20 minutes.

3 Thinly slice the cucumber lengthwise, using a vegetable peeler. Sprinkle with the salt and leave to drain for 30 minutes. Rinse well, dry on paper towels, and place in a bowl. (If using seaweed, pour on boiling water and soak for 10 minutes; drain, dry well, and add to the cucumber.)

4 Using a garlic crusher, squeeze out as much juice from the ginger as possible, and mix the ginger juice with the vinegar and sugar. Add to the cucumber, toss well, and set aside until required.

5 Preheat the grill. Remove the chicken from the marinade and thread onto the bamboo skewers. Grill for 6–7 minutes, turning and basting with the marinade until the chicken is cooked through.

6 Serve the chicken skewers hot with the cucumber salad.

Note Saké, or Japanese rice wine, is available from oriental food stores and some wine retailers. If unavailable, medium dry sherry may be substituted.

Japanese cooking uses few ingredients; flavors are light, and dishes are healthful and often quick to prepare.

Warm chicken and asparagus salad

10 ounces asparagus, trimmed
4 chicken breast fillets, cut into
  strips
1 tablespoon vegetable oil
salt and pepper
4 tablespoons fresh mint leaves
¼ pound baby spinach leaves

For the lemongrass dressing:
1 tablespoon sesame oil
1 tablespoon vegetable oil
1 teaspoon paprika
2 lemongrass stalks, thinly sliced
3 tablespoons lime juice
1 tablespoon honey
2 tablespoons light soy sauce

1 Preheat the broiler to medium. Blanch the asparagus in boiling water for
3 minutes; drain and pat dry.
2 Brush the chicken strips and asparagus with oil; and season with salt
and pepper. Place on the broiler rack and broil for 3–4 minutes on each side,
or until the chicken is cooked through.
3 Meanwhile, make the dressing. Gently heat the oils in a small pan. Add
the paprika and lemongrass, and cook for 1–2 minutes.
4 Arrange the mint and spinach leaves on plates, and top with the asparagus
and chicken.
5 Add the lime juice, honey, and soy sauce to the dressing, and slowly bring
to a simmer. Pour the warm dressing over the salad to serve.

Note Chargrill the chicken strips and asparagus, if you prefer.

An easy, elegant salad enhanced with a warm
oriental-flavored dressing.

Poussins stuffed with herb butter

Serves 6

6 spatchcocked poussins (see below)

For the herb butter

6 garlic cloves (unpeeled)

1½ sticks (10 tablespoons) unsalted butter, softened

3 tablespoons finely chopped fresh tarragon

3 tablespoons finely snipped fresh chives

salt and pepper

For the garnish

2 tablespoons roughly torn flat leaf parsley

1 Simmer the garlic cloves in water to cover for 6 minutes until softened; drain and cool slightly. Snip the root end, and squeeze out the garlic into a bowl. Crush and mix in the butter, tarragon, chives, and seasoning.

2 Gently ease up the skin on the breast and upper part of the poussins' legs with your fingers to make a pocket for the herb butter, taking care to avoid puncturing the skin. Spread the butter over the flesh under the skin, then press down the loosened skin.

3 Thread 2 wooden skewers crosswise through each bird to hold it flat (from wing through to the opposite leg). Set aside until ready to cook.

4 Preheat the broiler to medium and the oven to 250°F. Broil the poussins for 20–25 minutes, turning occasionally until golden and cooked through. Keep warm in the oven. Scatter with parsley to serve.

Note To spatchcock a bird, lay it flat on the worksurface, breast down, and cut along the backbone with a sharp knife or poultry shears. Remove the backbone and wishbone. Press down on the bird to flatten it.

Serve these young chickens on a mound of buttered saffron couscous. In summer, barbecue, rather than broil, the poussins.

Citrus roast chicken

1 oven-ready chicken, about
  3½ pounds
olive oil, for brushing
2 teaspoons five-pepper mix, crushed
3 tablespoons redcurrant jelly
juice of 1 pink grapefruit

pink grapefruit segments, to
  garnish

1 Preheat oven to 400°F. Brush the chicken with oil, then sprinkle with the crushed pepper and salt. Place breast side down in a non-metal shallow ovenproof dish. Roast for 45 minutes.

2 Melt the redcurrant jelly in a pan over a low heat. Add the grapefruit juice, and bring to the boil, stirring. Turn chicken breast side up and spoon half of the glaze over. Lower oven setting to 350°F, and roast chicken for another 45 minutes, or until cooked through, basting at intervals.

3 Transfer the chicken to a serving dish, cover loosely with foil, and rest in a warm place for 15 minutes. Skim off the oil from the pan juices, and heat until bubbling.

4 Serve the chicken garnished with grapefruit segments, with the pan juices as a gravy.

Notes To calculate roasting time, allow about 20 minutes per pound weight plus an extra 20 minutes at 400°F. To test that the chicken is thoroughly cooked, pierce the thickest part of the leg with a skewer, and make sure that the juices run clear, not at all pink.

An original roast—flavored with crushed five-pepper mix, a fresh grapefruit and redcurrant glaze.

Sesame roast chicken

1 oven-ready chicken, about
   3½ pounds
3 tablespoons sesame oil
3 tablespoons soy sauce

2–3 teaspoons grated fresh
   gingerroot
1 teaspoon sesame seeds

1 Preheat oven to 400°F. Mix the oil, soy sauce, and ginger together, and brush half inside and over the chicken.

2 Lay breast down in roasting pan, and roast for 45 minutes. Turn breast up and brush with more soy mixture. Roast for 20 minutes.

3 Brush again, sprinkle with sesame seeds, and roast for another 25 minutes or until cooked, reducing setting if browning too fast.

Note Roasting the chicken breast-side down to start with helps to keep the breast meat succulent and moist.

This oriental style roast is delicious served with ready-made plum sauce and a salad of shredded cucumber and green onion.

Mango and chicken salad

4 cooked chicken breasts (preferably roasted)
2 large mangoes, peeled, halved, and stoned
½ cup roasted cashew nuts
½ head of iceberg lettuce, shredded
For the dressing
½ cup coconut milk
½ teaspoon ground coriander
1 tablespoon Thai fish sauce
1 tablespoon soft brown sugar
2 green onions, finely sliced
1 tablespoon finely chopped fresh mint
2 teaspoons finely chopped fresh lemongrass
salt and pepper

1 First make the dressing. Put the ingredients in a small pan and heat gently until the sugar is dissolved. Remove from the heat and set aside.
2 Cut the chicken and mango flesh into cubes or slices, and place in a large bowl with the cashew nuts. Toss to mix.
3 Divide the shredded lettuce between 4 plates, and top with the chicken and mango mixture. Stir the dressing and pour over the salad to serve.

Variation Use papaws (papayas) instead of mangoes.

Scented mango, roast chicken, cashew nuts, and crisp lettuce in a Thai coconut dressing, flavored with fresh mint and lemongrass.

Aromatic chicken parcels

8 large chicken drumsticks or
   thighs, skinned
sea salt and pepper
24 large fresh basil leaves, or
   2 tablespoons chopped fresh basil
a little oil, for brushing

1 Preheat oven to 400°F.
2 Season the chicken generously with salt and pepper, then press 3 basil leaves onto each drumstick or thigh, or roll each chicken piece in chopped basil to coat.
3 Lightly oil the 4 baking parchment sheets in the center only. Place 2 chicken pieces on the oiled part of each piece of paper. Fold up the two short sides over the chicken and pleat them together at the top, then fold over the two loose ends and pleat to make a fairly secure parcel.
4 Place the parcels on a baking tray, and bake for about 30 minutes until the chicken is cooked through. Serve with vegetables.

Note For the parcels you will need 4 sheets of baking parchment, each about 12x9 inches.

Cooking herb-coated chicken in parcels seals in all of the flavor and moisture.

Pumpkin and chicken broth

1 tablespoon oil
4 shallots, minced
1 teaspoon grated fresh gingerroot
2 lemongrass stalks, minced
2 skinless chicken breast fillets
3 cups pumpkin flesh, cut into
   approx. ⅝-inch cubes

5 cups good-quality chicken stock
4 tablespoons chopped fresh basil
salt and pepper

1 Heat the oil in a large heavy-based pan, and fry the shallots until soft.
Add the ginger and lemongrass; stir-fry for 1 minute.
2 Add the chicken and cubed pumpkin flesh. Cook, stirring, for 1 minute.
3 Pour in the stock. Bring to the boil, cover and simmer for 10–15 minutes,
or until the chicken is cooked through and the pumpkin is tender. Stir in
the chopped basil, and check the seasoning before serving.

Serve this fragrant Thai broth as a lunch or
light supper, with plenty of crusty bread.

Smoky chicken wings

12 large chicken wings
2 tablespoons olive oil
juice of ½ lemon
2 teaspoons sweet chile sauce
1 teaspoon Pimenton (smoked
  Spanish paprika) or sweet paprika

1 tablespoon sun-dried tomato paste
  or ordinary tomato paste
1 garlic clove, crushed
salt and pepper
thyme sprigs, to garnish

1 Presoak 8 long wooden or bamboo skewers in cold water for 20 minutes.
Mix the olive oil, lemon juice, chile sauce, paprika, tomato paste, and garlic
together to form a thick sauce.

2 Preheat the broiler (or barbecue). Cut off the very tips of the chicken
wings. Thread 3 chicken wings onto 2 parallel skewers; repeat with the
remaining wings and skewers.

3 Broil (or barbecue) for 15 minutes, turning twice, then brush liberally
with the sauce. Broil (or barbecue) for another 10–15 minutes until cooked
through and nicely browned, turning and basting with the sauce from time
to time.

4 Season and garnish with thyme to serve. Eat the chicken wings with
your fingers!

Note The secret of these barbecued wings is to brush with the glaze toward
the end of cooking, rather than at the start, to avoid scorching them.

Broil or barbecue these spicy sweet-sour
glazed chicken wings. Serve with warm bread
and a tomato salad.

Deviled chicken

2 tablespoons olive oil
4 boneless chicken breasts (with skin)
2 garlic cloves, chopped
2 tablespoons balsamic vinegar
6 tablespoons dry white wine

4 tablespoons well flavored chicken stock
1 tablespoon sun-dried tomato paste
½ teaspoon mild chile powder
2 tablespoons chopped fresh parsley
salt and pepper

1 Heat the oil in a skillet, add the chicken, skin side down, and fry gently for 15 minutes, undisturbed.
2 Turn the chicken over, add the garlic, and fry gently for another 5–10 minutes until cooked through. Transfer to a warmed serving dish, and leave to rest in a warm place while making the sauce.
3 Pour the balsamic vinegar, wine, and stock into the pan, scraping up any sediment. Whisk in the tomato paste and chile powder. Let bubble until reduced and syrupy. Stir in the parsley and any juices from the chicken; taste and season. Pour the deviled sauce over the chicken to serve.

A rich and fiery sauce made in minutes with the pan juices and dark balsamic vinegar.

Stir fried chicken, bok choi and egg noodles

2 skinless chicken breast fillets
6 tablespoons dark soy sauce
2 garlic cloves, crushed
1 tablespoon cornstarch
1 tablespoon soft brown sugar
2 teaspoons grated fresh gingerroot
¼ pound medium Chinese egg
   noodles

2 tablespoons sunflower oil
2 carrots, cut into matchstick strips
4 tablespoons dry sherry
8 green onions, sliced diagonally
7 ounces bok choi, roughly shredded
6 ounces bean sprouts
4 tablespoons chopped fresh cilantro

1 Cut the chicken into strips, and mix with the soy sauce, garlic, cornstarch, sugar, and ginger. Cook the noodles according to the pack instructions.
2 Heat the oil in a wok, and stir-fry the carrot until starting to soften. Add the chicken mixture, and stir-fry for 2–3 minutes. Sprinkle in the sherry and allow to bubble until it is totally reduced.
3 Add the green onions, bok choi, and bean sprouts. Heat through, stirring, then add the drained egg noodles and chopped cilantro. Toss well to mix and serve immediately, in warmed bowls.

This aromatic, colorful stir-fry is quick to
ssemble and cook.

Enchiladas

2 tablespoons olive oil
2 red bell peppers, seeded and thinly
  sliced
2 red onions, sliced
3 cloves garlic, crushed
2 red chiles, seeded and sliced
2 teaspoons ground coriander
2 teaspoons ground cumin
4 chicken breast fillets, cut into
  strips

salt and pepper
8-ounce can refried beans
4 tablespoons chopped fresh cilantro
1¼ cup sour cream
8 flour tortillas
5 ounces sharp cheddar cheese,
  grated

1 Heat the oil in a large pan, then add the peppers, onions, garlic, and three-quarters of the chiles. Stir-fry over a high heat for about 8 minutes until softened.

2 Stir in the ground spices, then add the chicken strips and seasoning. Cook, covered, for 5 minutes.

3 Remove from the heat; stir in the refried beans, three-quarters of the fresh cilantro and 2 tablespoons of the sour cream.

4 Lay the tortillas on a work surface. Divide the chicken mixture between them, and roll up to enclose. Place in a large ovenproof dish, and top with the remaining sour cream. Scatter over the cheese, remaining chiles and cilantro. If preparing ahead, cover and chill for up to 2 days.

5 When ready to serve, preheat oven to 375°F. Cover the tortilla dish with foil and bake for 50 minutes. Remove the foil and bake for another 10–15 minutes until golden and piping hot. Serve with an avocado and lettuce salad.

Spicy Mexican tortillas are filled with chicken, refried beans and cilantro, then baked in sour cream with a cheese and chile topping.

Chicken on a bed of bay leaves

2 tablespoons olive oil
20 fresh bay leaves
4 skinless chicken breast fillets
salt and pepper

1 Heat the oil gently in a heavy-based pan or casserole. Cover the base
of the pan with a layer of bay leaves, then lay the chicken breast fillets
on top. Season, cover tightly, and cook for 10–12 minutes.
2 Turn the chicken breasts over, re-cover and cook for another 10 minutes or
until cooked through. Serve the chicken with the pan juices and vegetables
of your choice.

This unusual Italian way of cooking chicken
imparts a unique flavor.

Chorizo and chicken gumbo

3 tablespoons olive oil
2 tablespoons all-purpose flour
2 fresh bay leaves
1 large onion, minced
4 celery sticks, thickly sliced
1 tablespoon Cajun seasoning
1 teaspoon fresh thyme leaves
15-ounce can peeled tomatoes in
  juice

3 cups chicken stock
2 green bell peppers, seeded and
  cubed
5 ounces okra, trimmed (halved if
  large)
8 skinless chicken thighs
7-ounce piece chorizo sausage,
  skinned and diced
salt and pepper

1 Heat the oil in a large heavy-based pan or flameproof casserole. Stir
in the flour and bay leaves, and cook gently for about 5 minutes, stirring
frequently until the flour is a nutty brown color.
2 Tip in the onion and celery, and cook gently for 5 minutes. Stir in the
Cajun seasoning and thyme leaves.
3 Pour in the tomatoes and stock, then stir in all the remaining ingredients,
seasoning with salt and pepper to taste. Cover and simmer for 40 minutes
until the chicken is tender. If preparing ahead, cool and refrigerate for up
to 3 days.
4 When ready to serve, reheat on the cooktop until piping hot. Serve with
mixed basmati and wild rice or bread and a leafy salad.

Spicy Spanish chorizo gives this stew a rich
flavor. Okra is an authentic ingredient and its
sticky juices help to thicken the sauce.

Shrimp and chicken laksa

1 tablespoon vegetable oil
1 onion, minced
2 teaspoons grated fresh gingerroot
2 teaspoons crushed garlic
3 lemongrass stalks, minced
1 tablespoon ground coriander
2 teaspoons ground cumin
1 red chile, seeded and thinly sliced
4 boneless chicken thighs, skinned
   and cut into bite-size pieces

1¾ cup coconut milk
⅞ cup chicken stock
⅞ cup cooked, peeled tiger shrimp
6 tablespoons finely chopped fresh
   cilantro
salt and pepper
7 ounces medium egg noodles

1 Heat the oil in a large heavy-based pan, add the onion, ginger, garlic, and lemongrass, and cook gently until the onion is softened.
2 Add the spices and stir-fry for 1 minute, then add the chile and chicken. Stir-fry for 2–3 minutes, then pour in the coconut milk and stock. Bring to a simmer and cook gently for 15–20 minutes. Stir in the shrimp and cilantro leaves; season.
3 Meanwhile cook the noodles according to the pack instructions; drain well. Divide between serving bowls. Top with the shrimp mixture to serve.

Fragrant lemongrass, spicy red chile, fresh gingerroot, and pungent cilantro gives this Thai dish its distinctive character.

easy
meat

Honey, ginger, and orange duck kabobs

6 duck breast fillets, each about
  6 ounces
grated rind and juice of 1 orange
4 tablespoons clear honey
1 tablespoon dark soy sauce
1 teaspoon ground ginger
1 teaspoon chile powder

1 red and 1 yellow bell pepper,
  halved, cored, and seeded
For the garnish
toasted sesame seeds
shredded green onion

1 Remove the skin and fat from the duck breasts. Cut the meat into 1½-inch pieces, and put into a shallow, nonmetallic dish.

2 Mix together the orange rind and juice, honey, soy sauce, ginger, and chile powder. Drizzle the mixture over the meat, and turn to coat well.

3 Cut the peppers into 1½-inch squares and add to the meat. Toss well and leave to marinate for 30 minutes.

4 Preheat the broiler to high. Thread the duck and pepper pieces alternately onto 8 metal skewers.

5 Place the kabobs on the broiler rack and baste with the marinade. Broil for about 10 minutes, turning and basting from time to time, until the peppers are charred and the duck is evenly browned and cooked through.

6 Transfer the kabobs to warmed serving plates, allowing 2 per person. Sprinkle toasted sesame seeds over, and garnish with shredded green onion. Serve at once, accompanied by rice and a salad.

These tangy duck and sweet pepper kabobs are best served with Thai jasmine rice and a leafy salad.

Duck breasts with berry sauce

4 boneless duck breasts, each
  6–7 ounces
salt and pepper
juice of 1 orange
4 tablespoons redcurrant jelly

generous cup fresh or frozen mixed
  berries (red currants, blackberries,
  raspberries, and cherries)
½ teaspoon white wine vinegar

1 Preheat oven to 425°F.

2 Score the duck breast fat and rub with salt. Heat a large skillet over a medium-high heat. Add the duck breasts, skin side down, and cook for about 7 minutes until most of the fat is rendered from under the skin.

3 Turn the duck breasts over, and seal briefly on the other side, then transfer to a rack over a roasting pan, and roast for 15–20 minutes.

4 Meanwhile pour off the fat from the skillet, and wipe clean with paper towels. Add the orange juice, redcurrant jelly, berry fruits, and wine vinegar to the pan. Season with salt and pepper to taste, and let bubble until the sauce is syrupy.

5 Leave the duck to rest for a few minutes before carving into slices. Arrange on warmed serving plates, and spoon the berry sauce over. Serve with sautéed potatoes and green beans or snow peas.

Assorted berry fruits in an orange and redcurrant sauce cut the richness of duck to delicious effect.

Butterflied lamb with a spiced yoghurt crust

Serves 6–8

4½-pound butterfied leg of lamb
1 tablespoon dried green
  peppercorns, crushed
1 tablespoon black peppercorns,
  crushed

3 garlic cloves, crushed
⅝ cup Greek yogurt

1 Lay the meat skin side down, and score the thicker parts as necessary to make it an even thickness. Make slits all over the surface.
2 Mix the crushed peppercorns, garlic, and yogurt together, and rub this mixture all over the cut surface of the lamb. Lay the meat in a shallow dish, cover, and then leave to marinate in the fridge for at least 1 hour, preferably overnight.
3 Lift the lamb onto a foil-lined broiler rack, and cook under a medium-hot grill for 20 minutes each side, until medium.
4 Leave the meat to rest for 10 minutes, then carve into long, thin slices. Serve with yogurt, flavored with chopped mint, and grilled naan bread.

Note To barbecue, cook over medium-hot coals for 15–20 minutes, then turn and cook for another 15–20 minutes. Ask your butcher to butterfly a leg of lamb for this recipe (i.e. bone the meat and open it out flat).

Boneless flattened leg of lamb, rubbed with crushed peppercorns, garlic, and Greek yogurt, and broiled until meltingly tender.

Lamb chops with sweet potatoes and garlic

Illustrated on previous pages

4 loin lamb chops or 8 lamb cutlets
4 tablespoons olive oil
2¼ pounds sweet potatoes, peeled and cubed
2 red onions, cut into wedges
8 garlic cloves (unpeeled)
1 tablespoon light muscovado sugar

juice of 1 lemon
1 small lemon, halved and thinly sliced
1 tablespoon fresh thyme leaves, plus 8 sprigs
salt and pepper

1 Trim the lamb of any excess fat. Preheat oven to 425°F.

2 Heat the olive oil in a large skillet. Add the sweet potato cubes, onion wedges, garlic, and sugar, and fry, stirring, over a high heat for about 5 minutes until the vegetables start to soften and caramelize. Transfer to a roasting pan.

3 Add the lemon juice, lemon slices, thyme leaves, and seasoning, then top with the lamb chops and thyme sprigs.

4 Roast in the oven for 25–30 minutes until the lamb is cooked and the sweet potatoes are tender. Serve garnished with remaining thyme and accompanied by spinach.

Sweet potatoes are sautéed with lemon, red onions, and fresh thyme, then topped with lamb chops and quick roasted.

Lamb tagine

2 tablespoons vegetable oil
1 large onion, minced
2 garlic cloves, finely chopped
2¼ pounds boned shoulder of lamb,
    cut into 2-inch cubes
1 teaspoon saffron threads
1 teaspoon ground ginger

3¾ cups lamb stock or water
1½ cups ready-to-eat dried prunes
1½ cups ready-to-eat dried apricots
2 teaspoons ground cinnamon
2 tablespoons clear honey
salt and pepper

1 Heat the oil in a heavy-based pan or flameproof casserole, and sauté the onion and garlic until soft. Add the meat and fry, turning occasionally, until evenly browned.

2 Add the saffron, ginger, and stock or water, and stir well. Cover and simmer gently for 1½ hours or until the meat is tender, adding a little hot water if the stew appears to be a little too dry.

3 Add the prunes, apricots, cinnamon, and honey. Season with salt and pepper to taste, re-cover, and simmer for another 15 minutes.

4 Taste and adjust the seasoning. Serve with steamed couscous or rice, and a salad or green vegetable.

A wonderful Moroccan stew of lamb and dried fruit, enriched with saffron, ginger, cinnamon, and honey.

Creole meatballs

1¼ pound lean ground lamb
1 onion, minced
3 tablespoons all-purpose flour
1 teaspoon hot paprika
salt and pepper
oil for shallow-frying
For the creole sauce
1 tablespoon vegetable oil
1 onion, minced

2 red bell peppers, cored, seeded, and
   chopped
3 garlic cloves, finely chopped
15-ounce can chopped tomatoes
1 bay leaf
⅛ pound fresh pineapple, roughly
   cubed
scant 1 cup water

1 For the meatballs, put the ground lamb, onion, flour, paprika, and
seasoning in a bowl, and mix thoroughly. With wet hands, divide the
mixture equally into 16 pieces and shape into balls.

2 Heat the oil in a large skillet; carefully fry the meatballs, turning until evenly
browned. Drain on crumpled paper towels; set aside. Heat oven to 400°F.

3 To make the creole sauce, heat the oil in a skillet, and gently fry the onion
until softened. Add the red peppers and garlic; stir-fry for 1 minute. Add the
remaining ingredients, season well, and bring to the boil, stirring.

4 Put the meatballs in a shallow ovenproof dish. Pour the sauce over, and
bake in the oven for 20–25 minutes. Serve with plain boiled rice and a crisp
green salad.

Tender lamb meatballs cooked in a mildly
spiced creole sauce with fresh pineapple and
red bell peppers.

Bobotie

Serves 6–8

1 tablespoon vegetable oil

1 large onion, minced

2 garlic cloves, minced

2¼ pound lean ground lamb

2 teaspoons ground coriander

1 teaspoon ground cumin

1 teaspoon paprika

1½ cups fresh white breadcrumbs

2 tablespoons white wine vinegar

2 eggs, beaten

4 tablespoons golden raisins

4 tablespoons apricot jam

salt and pepper

For the topping

2 eggs

scant 1 cup heavy cream

2 tablespoons chopped fresh cilantro
  leaves

cilantro sprigs, to garnish

1 Line a 9-inch springform cake pan with nonstick baking parchment.
Preheat oven to 350°F.

2 Heat the oil in a large nonstick skillet, add the onion and garlic, and fry
gently until lightly browned. Add the meat, and fry, stirring occasionally,
until browned.

3 Take off the heat and mix in the spices, breadcrumbs, vinegar, beaten eggs,
raisins, jam, and salt to taste. Turn the mixture into the pan, and spread evenly.

4 For the topping, beat the eggs and cream together in a bowl; season well,
then pour the mixture over the meat. Scatter the cilantro over the surface.
Stand the cake pan on a baking sheet and bake for 1 hour.

5 Carefully unmold the bobotie. Serve cut into wedges, and garnish with
some cilantro.

Serve this spicy meatloaf from South Africa
with yogurt and a salad.

Rump steaks with wilted arugula

4 rump steaks, each 6 ounces
For the marinade
5 tablespoons red wine
2 garlic cloves, crushed
3 tablespoons olive oil
salt and pepper

For the aioli
2 garlic cloves, peeled and crushed
1 egg yolk
3 tablespoons walnut oil
scant ½ cup light olive oil
lemon juice, to taste
To serve
¼ pound arugula leaves

1 In a shallow dish, mix together the wine, garlic, olive oil, and seasoning. Add the rump steaks and turn to coat well. Cover and leave to marinate for 30 minutes.

2 Meanwhile, make the aioli. Pound the garlic with 1 teaspoon salt in a small bowl. Stir in the egg yolk. Gradually whisk in the oils, a few drops at a time. Once half the oil is incorporated, add a squeeze of lemon juice. Whisk in remaining oil in a thin, steady stream. Taste and season, or add lemon juice as required.

3 Remove steaks from marinade, and pat dry on paper towels. Brush with a little olive oil. Preheat broiler to medium. Put the steaks on the broiler rack, and cook for 3 minutes each side, or to taste.

4 Serve each steak topped with a pile of arugula leaves and accompanied by the aioli.

Note To barbecue, cook over medium-hot coals for 2–3 minutes per side, or to taste.

Tender, marinated rump steaks served topped with rocket and accompanied by a delicious aioli – made with walnut oil.

Horseradish-crusted roast beef

Serves 4–6

3 pounds boned, rolled rib of beef

salt and pepper

3 tablespoons fresh breadcrumbs

2 tablespoons hot horseradish sauce

2 teaspoons grated horseradish

1 Preheat oven to 400°F. Pat the meat dry with paper towels, if necessary. Season with salt and pepper.

2 Mix the remaining ingredients together to make a paste, then spread over the meat.

3 Put the meat into a roasting pan, and roast in the oven for 45 minutes. Reduce oven setting to 350°F, and roast for another 45 minutes. Rest in a warm place for 10 minutes before carving.

Note Always bring a roasting joint to room temperature before cooking, since this will affect the timing.

The best partner for a beautifully cooked roast is a very sharp carving knife—it will make the meat go much further!

Beef with bacon, thyme, and garlic

Serves 4–6

3 pounds boned, rolled sirloin or rib of beef

3 ounces smoked bacon lardoons (bacon cut crosswise into thin strips)

3 garlic cloves, cut lengthwise into wedges

15 small fresh thyme sprigs

salt and pepper

olive oil, for basting

1 Preheat oven to 400°F. Cut about 15 slits in the beef with a sharp knife and insert a piece of bacon, a wedge of garlic, and a thyme sprig into each one.

2 Season the joint all over with salt and pepper, and rub with a little olive oil.

3 Roast in the oven for 1½–2 hours until cooked to your preference. Leave to rest in a warm place for 10 minutes before carving.

Note For a succulent roast, look for a joint with a good marbling of fat, since this will help to keep the meat moist during roasting.

Boned and rolled sirloin or rib of beef studded with lardoons, garlic slivers, and thyme sprigs.

Corned beef hash patties

4 tablespoons sunflower oil
1 onion, halved and thinly sliced
1 red bell pepper, quartered, cored, seeded, and thinly sliced
2 garlic cloves, sliced
1¼ pound potatoes (unpeeled), coarsely grated

6 large eggs
2 teaspoons Worcestershire sauce
dash of Tabasco sauce
salt and pepper
4 green onions, finely chopped
8-ounce can corned beef, diced

1 Heat half of the oil in a large skillet, add the onion, red pepper, garlic, and potatoes, and fry, stirring, for 8 minutes until softened.
2 In a large bowl, beat 2 eggs with the Worcestershire sauce, Tabasco, and seasoning. Add the potato mixture, green onions, and corned beef; mix together thoroughly. Divide into 4 portions and shape roughly into patties.
3 Heat the remaining oil in the skillet. Add the potato patties, cover, and cook for 10 minutes. Turn the potato cakes over, and cook for another 5 minutes.
4 Meanwhile, poach the remaining 4 eggs in boiling salted water for 3 minutes or until cooked to your liking; lift out with a slotted spoon.
5 Serve the patties topped with the poached eggs, and an extra few drops of Tabasco, if liked.

Note If you do not have a skillet large enough to hold all four patties, use two pans, rather then cook in batches.

This unusual, tasty supper also makes a great Sunday brunch. Serve with a refreshing leafy salad.

Bean casserole with chorizo

1½ cups dried pinto beans

⅝ cup dried butter beans

1 tablespoon olive oil

1 pound small white onions, peeled

½ pound thick smoked ham steak, cubed

7 ounces chorizo sausage, skinned and cut into chunks

1 each green and orange bell pepper, cored, seeded and cut into chunks

3 cups passata or drained and sieved canned tomatoes

2 cups chicken stock

3 tablespoons molasses

2 tablespoons wholegrain mustard

4 fresh bay leaves

1 tablespoon fresh thyme leaves

1 teaspoon paprika

1 Soak the pinto and butter beans separately in plenty of cold water overnight.

2 The next day, rinse the beans ad place in separate large pans. Add fresh cold water to cover, and bring to the boil. Fast boil the butter beans for 10 minutes; pinto beans for 20 minutes. Drain.

3 Heat the oil in a large pan. Add the whole onions and fry over a medium heat for about 5 minutes, stirring frequently.

4 Add the ham, chorizo, and peppers, and cook, stirring, for a few minutes. Pour in the passata and stock, then stir in the beans, molasses, mustard, herbs, and paprika. Cover and simmer gently, stirring frequently, for 45 minutes or until the beans are tender.

5 If preparing ahead, cool, then cover and refrigerate for up to 2 days, or freeze.

6 To serve, defrost at cool room temperature overnight (if frozen). Reheat in a pan until piping hot. Serve with garlic bread and a salad.

Molasses and spicy chorizo sausages give this rustic dish a wonderful depth of flavor.

Mexican beef stew with lime and chile

3 tablespoons vegetable oil
1½ pound lean ground beef
1 large onion, minced
1 green chile, thinly sliced
4 tablespoons lime juice
15-ounce can chopped tomatoes
2 Granny Smith apples, peeled,
   cored, and roughly chopped

2 tablespoons capers
salt and pepper
3 large potatoes, peeled and cut into
   ¾-inch cubes
1 garlic clove, finely chopped
2 teaspoons ground cumin
grated cheddar cheese, to garnish

1 Heat 2 tablespoons oil in a large heavy-based skillet. Add the beef and onion, and fry, stirring, until the meat is browned.

2 Add the chile, lime juice, tomatoes, apples, and capers. Lower the heat, cover with a tight-fitting lid, and simmer for 25 minutes or until the meat is tender. Season to taste.

3 Parboil the potatoes in salted water for 10 minutes; drain thoroughly.

4 Heat the remaining oil in a large, nonstick skillet. Add the potatoes, garlic, and cumin, and fry, stirring, until golden brown.

5 Divide the spiced potatoes between warmed plates, and top with the stew. Sprinkle with some grated cheese, and serve with tortillas or crusty bread and a salad.

Known as picadillo in Mexico, this unusual stew is flavored with fresh chile, lime juice, apples, and cumin. It is served on a bed of fried potatoes and topped with cheese.

Penne with venison and ceps

½ cup dried ceps, rinsed and chopped
⅝ cup boiling water
2 tablespoons olive oil
2 large onions, halved and sliced
1½ pounds ground venison
⅝ cup red wine
3 tablespoons tomato paste
1 tablespoon chopped fresh
  marjoram
salt and pepper

For the pasta and sauce
6 ounces penne or other pasta
  shapes
4 tablespoons butter
⅜ cup flour
2½ cups milk
1 egg, beaten
6 ounces sharp cheddar, grated
1 slice of bread, diced

1 Soak the dried ceps in the boiling water for about 15 minutes.
2 Heat the oil in a large pan, and gently fry the onions for 8–10 minutes, until golden. Add the meat and stir-fry until browned.
3 Pour in the wine, and add the mushrooms with their soaking liquid. Stir in the tomato paste, marjoram, and seasoning, cover and simmer for 10 minutes.
4 Cook the pasta in a large pan of boiling water for 10 minutes or until al dente; drain.
5 Meanwhile put the butter, flour, and milk in a pan, and whisk over a low heat until smooth and thickened. Stir in the pasta, season, and let cool slightly, then beat in the egg and two-thirds of the cheese.
6 Spread the meat mixture in a large ovenproof dish. Spoon the pasta and sauce over, then top with the bread and the rest of the cheese. If preparing ahead, cover and chill for up to 2 days, or freeze.
7 To serve, preheat oven to 375°F. Bake the pasta dish in the oven for 40 minutes until bubbling and golden. Serve with a leafy salad.

Ground venison in a rich stock flavored with dried mushrooms and fresh marjoram, baked under a cheesy pasta topping.

Venison steaks with juniper and ginger

4 venison steaks, each 6 ounces
olive oil, for brushing
salt and pepper

For the butter

1½ sticks (12 tablespoons) unsalted
   butter
1 tablespoon finely chopped fresh
   gingerroot

3 juniper berries, minced
1 teaspoon coarse salt

1 For the flavored butter, beat the butter in a bowl until very soft, then beat in the ginger, juniper berries, and salt. Shape into a log, wrap, and chill for 1 hour until firm.

2 Preheat broiler to medium. Brush the steaks with olive oil and season well. Place on the broiler rack and broil for 3–4 minutes on each side.

3 Serve the venison steaks topped with slices of the flavored butter.

Broiled lean venison steaks topped with slices of savory butter, flavored with fresh gingerroot, salt, and juniper berries.

Spiced pork scallops with apricots

Illustrated on previous pages

Serves 2–3

1 pound pork tenderloin, cut into
 ½-inch slices
1 teaspoon powdered cloves
salt and pepper

6 fresh apricots, stoned and
 quartered
3 whole cloves
6 tablespoons water
2 teaspoons clear honey

1 Lay the pork slices between sheets of waxed paper and beat with
a rolling pin to flatten. Sprinkle with the ground cloves, salt, and pepper.
2 Heat a large nonstick skillet until very hot. Cook the pork in batches for
about 1 minute each side until tender; transfer to a warmed dish, cover, and
keep warm in a low oven while cooking the sauce.
3 Add the apricots and whole cloves to the pan, and cook, shaking the pan,
for 2–3 minutes until they are lightly singed. Add the water and honey,
scraping up the sediment. Continue to cook until the apricots are softened
but still hold their shape, adding a little more water if needed.
4 Serve the meat topped with the apricots and pan juices. Accompany with
green beans or steamed zucchini.

Variations Use fresh plums or crisp apple wedges instead of apricots.

Tender pork fillet, beaten thin, cooks quickly
without losing its juiciness. Fresh apricots
spiced with cloves are the perfect foil.

French-style bacon steaks

1½ tablespoons sunflower oil
4 slices Canadian bacon, approx.
 ¼ inch thick
2 small red apples, cored and cut
 into wedges
2 tablespoons calvados or brandy

1 teaspoon green peppercorns in
 brine, crushed
2 teaspoons Dijon mustard
⅞ cup crème fraîche

1 Heat the oil in a large skillet, and fry the bacon steaks for about 5 minutes, turning once. Lift from the pan; set aside.

2 Add the apples to the pan, and sauté for 1 minute or until beginning to color. Add the calvados, then stir in the peppercorns, mustard, and crème fraîche to make a creamy sauce.

3 Return the bacon steaks to the pan to heat through before serving. Serve with mashed potatoes and stir-fried cabbage.

A chunky apple sauce spiked with calvados, Dijon mustard, and green peppercorns cuts the richness of smoked Canadian bacon steaks.

Spiced crisp side pork

Serves 4–6

2¾–3-pound piece fresh side pork, boned

salt

1 teaspoon Thai seven-spice mix

10 ounces shallots, finely sliced

6 garlic cloves, minced

2 fat red chiles, seeded and finely chopped

2 tablespoons sunflower oil

4 tablespoons clear honey

⅓ cup white wine

3 tablespoons dark soy sauce

cilantro sprigs, to garnish

1 Using a very sharp knife, deeply score the pork skin through to the fat at ½-inch intervals. Rub in plenty of salt, and leave to draw out moisture for 1–1⅓ hours.

2 Preheat oven to 400°F. Dry the pork skin well with paper towels, and rub in the spice mix. Place in a shallow roasting pan and roast for 25 minutes. Mix the shallots, garlic, and chiles with the oil.

3 With a spoon, insert the shallot mixture under the pork and roast for 50 minutes or until the skin is very crisp.

4 Brush with 2 tablespoons honey and return to the oven for 10 minutes. Brush with another 1 tablespoon honey; roast for a final 10 minutes.

5 Transfer the pork and shallots to a serving plate, and rest in a warm place until the sauce is ready. Pour off the fat from the pan, place on a burner and add the wine, soy, and remaining honey, stirring to deglaze.

6 Cut the meat into squares. Serve on a bed of rice, with the sauce and shallots. Garnish with cilantro sprigs.

This is perfect with steamed bok choi and sticky rice. Buy organic pork if you can—its thick skin is easier to score.

Pork and prosciutto madeira meatballs

Illustrated on previous pages

12 ounces ground pork
2½ ounces prosciutto
1 large garlic clove, crushed
thin slice white bread
salt and pepper
1 medium egg

2 tablespoons sunflower oil
4 tablespoons Madeira
½ cup pork or chicken stock
6 sage leaves, shredded
⅝ cup heavy cream
1 pound dried linguine or spaghetti

1 Put the ground pork and prosciutto in a food processor and pulse briefly to chop the ham. Add the garlic, bread, ½ teaspoon salt, a generous grinding of pepper, and the egg. Process until well mixed.

2 Divide the mixture into 4 pieces, then shape 6 meatballs from each portion.

3 Heat the oil in a large skillet, and fry the meatballs, turning, until golden. Add the Madeira and bubble until reduced by half.

4 Pour in the stock, stir in the sage, and season. Simmer gently for 5 minutes, then stir in the cream.

5 Meanwhile, cook the linguine in a large pan of boiling salted water for 10 minutes until
al dente. Drain and toss with the meatballs and sauce. Serve with steamed Savoy cabbage.

These meatballs are surprisingly quick to make and taste superb.

Glazed ham and mango pockets

2 ham steaks, each ¾ pound
olive oil, for brushing
salt and pepper
For the glaze
2 tablespoons fine-cut orange
  marmalade
finely grated rind and juice of 1 lime

For the salsa
1 large mango, halved, peeled, and
  stoned
finely grated rind and juice of 1 lime
1 small red chile, seeded and
  chopped
2 tablespoons chopped fresh cilantro

1 For the glaze, warm the marmalade together with the lime rind and juice until melted.

2 Cut 4 thin slices from the mango; chop the rest. Mix the chopped mango with the remaining salsa ingredients; set aside.

3 Cut each steak in half crosswise and remove the bone. Cut a horizontal slit in each straight side, and slip in a slice of mango; secure with a toothpick. Brush with olive oil, and season well.

4 Preheat broiler to medium. Put the steaks on the broiler rack and broil for 5 minutes each side, brushing with glaze for the last minute on each side. Serve with the mango salsa.

Bacon chops are stuffed with a slice of mango, flavored with a tangy citrus glaze, then served with a mango salsa spiked with chile.

Hickory'n'maple ribs

8 meaty pork ribs, about 3 pounds
  in total
For the marinade
½ cup maple syrup
3 tablespoons hickory barbecue sauce

juice of 1 small lemon
1 tablespoon sweet chile sauce
2 garlic cloves, crushed

1 Put the pork ribs in a shallow non-metallic dish. Mix all the marinade
ingredients together in a bowl, then pour the mixture over the ribs and turn
to coat well. Cover and leave to marinate in the fridge for up to 2 days.
2 Preheat oven to 375°F. Transfer the ribs to a large, shallow roasting pan,
and baste with the marinade. Cover the pan loosely with foil, and bake for
40 minutes, then uncover and bake for another 40 minutes, basting
occasionally, until the meat is tender.
3 Serve the pork ribs accompanied by baked potatoes and coleslaw or warm
bread and a leafy green salad.

Variation Replace the marinade with a hot, spicy sauce. Mix together
6 tablespoons tomato ketchup, 4 tablespoons Worcestershire sauce,
2 tablespoons Dijon mustard, 4 tablespoons muscovado sugar, and a dash
of Tabasco sauce. Marinate the ribs in the mixture and cook as above. Serve
with garlic bread and a salad.

Smoky hickory sauce and maple syrup
enhance meaty spareribs to delicious effect.

easy
vegetables
and
salads

Sabzi pulao

2 cups basmati rice
2 tablespoons vegetable oil
1 onion, halved and thinly sliced
6 cardamom pods
6 cloves
1 cinnamon stick
½ pound mushrooms, roughly
   chopped

2 carrots, cut into cubes
1 red bell pepper, cored, seeded, and
   roughly chopped
1½ cups frozen peas
large pinch saffron threads, soaked
   in 2 teaspoons hot water
salt and pepper
crisp fried onion slices, to garnish

1 Rinse the rice in a large sieve under cold running water until the water
is clear; drain thoroughly.
2 Heat the oil in a large heavy-based pan, and sauté the onion over a medium
heat until lightly browned.
3 Add the cardamom pods, cloves, and cinnamon. Stir-fry for 1 minute, then
add the rice, and fry, stirring, for another 1 minute. Add the vegetables and
stir well.
4 Stir in 3¾ cups boiling water, the infused saffron, and seasoning. Cover
tightly. Simmer on a very low heat for 15 minutes.
5 Leave to stand, covered, for 10 minutes then fluff up the rice with a fork.
Serve garnished with crisp fried onions.

Serve this one-pot meal with hot pickles,
yogurt, and a cucumber and tomato salsa.

Stuffed beefsteak tomatoes

Illustrated on previous pages

Serves 2

4 large beefsteak or marmande
  tomatoes
⅝ cup dried pastina (small soup
  pasta)
salt and pepper
1 tablespoon olive oil

1 red onion, diced
1 garlic clove, crushed
2 teaspoons finely chopped fresh
  oregano
¼ pound mushrooms, diced
1 ounces Parmesan or pecorino
  cheese, finely grated

1 Preheat oven to 350°F. Cut off the tops of the tomatoes; set aside for
"lids." Using a teaspoon, scoop out the tomato seeds and cores to leave
½-inch thick shells.
2 Add the pasta to a pan of boiling salted water and cook until al dente.
Drain and rinse in cold water to arrest cooking; drain thoroughly.
3 Heat the olive oil in a pan, add the onion, and cook gently for 5 minutes
until softened but not colored. Add the garlic and cook for 2–3 minutes. Add
the oregano and mushrooms and fry for another 3–5 minutes. Allow to cool
slightly. Add grated cheese, pasta, and seasoning to taste; mix well.
4 Spoon the mushroom filling into the hollowed-out tomatoes, then replace
the tomato lids. Carefully transfer to an ovenproof dish, and bake for about
30 minutes, until the tomatoes are quite soft but still holding their shape.
Serve hot.

Juicy giant baked tomatoes filled with small
pasta, mushrooms, Parmesan, and oregano
make a tempting vegetarian meal.

Vegetable pie with Parmesan crust

For the vegetable filling
1¼ cups vegetable stock
1 fennel bulb, halved and sliced
3 leeks, sliced
3 carrots, sliced
3 zucchini, thickly sliced
3 tablespoons pesto
salt and pepper

For the Parmesan topping
1¼ cups self-rising flour
6 tablespoons butter, in pieces
1 cup fresh breadcrumbs
¼ pound Parmesan, freshly grated
4 tablespoons buttermilk (or half
    yogurt-half milk)

1 Preheat oven to 400°F. Bring the stock to the boil in a pan. Add the fennel, leeks, and carrots, cover and simmer for 10 minutes. Stir in the zucchini, pesto and seasoning to taste; cook for 5 minutes.
2 For the topping, tip the flour into a food processor, add the butter with a little seasoning, and process until incorporated.
3 Add the breadcrumbs and Parmesan to the processor, and pulse until evenly mixed, then add the buttermilk (or yogurt and milk) and process briefly until the mixture forms small clumps.
4 Spoon the vegetables into a 2½-quart ovenproof dish, and cover with the topping. Bake for 20–25 minutes until the topping is firm and golden. Serve with a leafy salad.

Pesto-enriched vegetables topped with a savory crumbly piecrust.

Radicchio, asparagus, and black beans

1 pound 2 ounces thin asparagus, trimmed to 5-inch lengths
2 radicchio, each cut into 6 wedges
4 garlic cloves, crushed
½ teaspoon dried chile flakes
8 tablespoons extra-virgin olive oil
salt and pepper

1⅓ cups cooked black beans (see note), or canned black, aduki, or red kidney beans
4 teaspoons balsamic vinegar

1 Put the asparagus and radicchio in a large shallow dish. Add the garlic, chile flakes, 4 tablespoons oil, and seasoning. Turn the vegetables to coat well.
2 Preheat a grill pan or heavy-based skillet over a medium heat, then cook the asparagus for 2 minutes on each side. Return to the dish.
3 Add the radicchio to the pan, and cook for 1 minute each side; add to the asparagus.
4 Put the black beans in a pan with some of their liquid. Warm through, then drain and add to the vegetables. Toss to mix, and check the seasoning.
5 Serve warm or cold, drizzled with the balsamic vinegar and remaining oil.

Note To obtain this weight of cooked beans, soak ⅝ cup dried black beans in cold water overnight. Drain, put into a pan, and cover with fresh water. Bring to the boil, and boil fast for 10 minutes, then lower the heat and simmer for 1½ hours or until tender.

This wonderful combination of flavors is perfect for a vegetarian meal. Serve warm or cold, with chargrilled flat bread if you like.

"Bubble and squeak" chorizo cake

Illustrated on previous pages

Serves 3–4

2¼ pounds potatoes, peeled and
  cubed
1 pound green cabbage, cored and
  shredded
2 leeks, thinly sliced
1 teaspoon salt
1 teaspoon coarsely ground black
  pepper

4 tablespoons butter
scant 1 cup milk
5 ounces chorizo sausage, skinned
  and chopped (optional)
2 tablespoons sunflower oil
chopped parsley, to garnish

1 Add the potatoes to a large pan of boiling salted water, bring to the boil, and position a steamer on top. Put the cabbage and leeks in the steamer, and cook for 20 minutes.

2 Drain the potatoes, and mash with the seasoning, butter, and milk until smooth and creamy. Stir in the cabbage, leeks, and chorizo sausage, if using. Allow to cool. (If preparing ahead, cover and chill.)

3 To cook, heat 1 tablespoon oil in a large heavy-based skillet. Add the potato mixture and press down to make a cake. Fry over a medium heat for 10 minutes.

4 Turn the cake out onto a large plate. Heat the remaining oil in the skillet, then slide the potato cake back into the pan and fry the other side for 5–10 minutes until golden and heated through. Serve at once, scattered with plenty of chopped parsley.

Spanish chorizo adds a unique flavor to this traditional British dish, but it can be omitted for vegetarians.

Cracked wheat pilaf, chestnuts and fennel

4 red onions, peeled with root end
intact
4 small fennel bulbs, trimmed with
root end intact
6 tablespoons olive oil
salt and pepper
1⅓ cups cracked wheat (bulgur
wheat)

3 cups well flavored vegetable stock
(preferably homemade)
1 cup cooked peeled chestnuts
3 tablespoons chopped flat leaf
parsley

1 Preheat oven to 425°F. Cut each onion and fennel bulb lengthwise into
6–8 pieces. Place on a baking tray and drizzle with half of the oil. Season
with salt and pepper, and turn well to coat the vegetables with the oil.
2 Rinse the cracked wheat, and drain well. Heat 2 tablespoons oil in a heavy-
based flameproof casserole. Add the cracked wheat and stir to coat with the
oil. Pour in the stock and bring to the boil. Lower the heat, cover, and
simmer gently for 15–20 minutes.
3 Meanwhile, roast the vegetables in the oven for 20 minutes.
4 When the cracked wheat is ready, turn off the heat, remove the lid, and
cover with a clean dish towel or muslin.
5 Add the chestnuts to the vegetables, turn to coat with oil, and return to the
oven for another 5 minutes. Fold the vegetables into the cracked wheat with
the remaining 1 tablespoon oil and the chopped parsley to serve.

Variation Serve the pilaf cold, with a herb vinaigrette folded through.

A simple, flexible vegetarian meal. Try using a
mixture of herbs, add canned aduki beans, or
scatter with toasted pine nuts.

Vietnamese salad

Illustrated on previous pages

4 tablespoons lime juice
3 tablespoons superfine sugar
salt and pepper
1 red onion, halved and finely sliced
¼ white or Savoy cabbage (approx.
   9 ounces), very finely shredded
1 large carrot, roughly grated
2 cooked boneless chicken breasts,
   skinned

2 tablespoons vegetable oil
3 tablespoons fresh torn mint leaves
2 tablespoons fresh torn cilantro
   leaves
1 tablespoon roasted peanuts,
   chopped

1 Mix the lime juice, sugar, ½ teaspoon salt, and ½ teaspoon pepper in a
bowl. Add the onion and leave to marinate for 30 minutes.
2 In a large, shallow serving bowl, toss the cabbage and carrot together.
3 Cut the chicken into strips, and add to the salad with the onion, marinade,
and oil. Toss well to mix.
4 Just before serving, fold in the mint and cilantro and then scatter the
peanuts over.

Light, crisp cabbage salad, also known
as Vietnamese coleslaw.

Spiced okra and potato stew

1 pound 2 ounces potatoes, peeled
2 tablespoons vegetable oil
1 onion, halved and thinly sliced
2 garlic cloves, finely chopped
1-inch piece fresh gingerroot, finely
  chopped
1 red chile, halved and finely sliced
2 teaspoons cumin seeds
½ teaspoon turmeric

2 teaspoons ground coriander
1¼ cups vegetable stock or water
15-ounce can chopped tomatoes
1 pound small okra, tips trimmed
  (see note)
salt and pepper
3 tablespoons chopped fresh cilantro
  leaves

1 Cut the potato into 1-inch cubes. Heat the oil in a large pan, add the onion, and cook gently for 10–15 minutes until soft and golden. Add the garlic, ginger, chile, and spices; fry, stirring, for 1 minute. Add the potatoes and mix well.
2 Pour in the stock and bring to the boil. Lower the heat, cover, and simmer for 5 minutes.
3 Stir in the tomatoes and cook briskly for 5 minutes, then add the okra. Season well with salt and pepper, cover and simmer gently for 15 minutes, stirring occasionally. Off the heat, stir in the chopped cilantro. Serve with warm naan bread.

Note To trim okra, remove a small piece from each end. Do not cut right into the pods, or you will release the sticky juices inside and the stew will acquire an unpleasant glutinous texture during cooking.

A delicious, spicy stew flavored with ginger, cumin, chile, and cilantro.

Warm mushroom, ham, and sweet potato salad

Serves 2

2 tablespoons butter

1 small sweet potato, peeled and diced

¼ pound small chestnut mushrooms, halved

10 wafter-thin slices Black Forest ham, each slice halved

2 ounces baby spinach leaves

small bunch watercress sprigs

For the dressing

3 tablespoons extra-virgin olive oil

1 tablespoon tarragon or red wine vinegar

1 garlic clove, crushed

1 teaspoon chopped fresh tarragon

1 tablespoon chopped fresh basil

salt and pepper

To garnish

basil sprigs

1 Melt the butter in a skillet, add the sweet potato, and fry, stirring frequently, for 8–10 minutes, until tender and golden.

2 Meanwhile, mix the dressing ingredients together in a bowl, seasoning with salt and pepper to taste.

3 Remove sweet potato from the pan; keep warm. Add the mushrooms to the pan, and fry for 3–4 minutes until softened. Add the ham and cook for 1–2 minutes.

4 Put the spinach and watercress on serving plates. Scatter with the mushrooms, ham, and sweet potato croûtons. Drizzle with the dressing and serve garnished with basil.

Note If Black Forest ham is unobtainable, use Parma ham instead.

A substantial warm salad, topped with sweet potato croûtons.

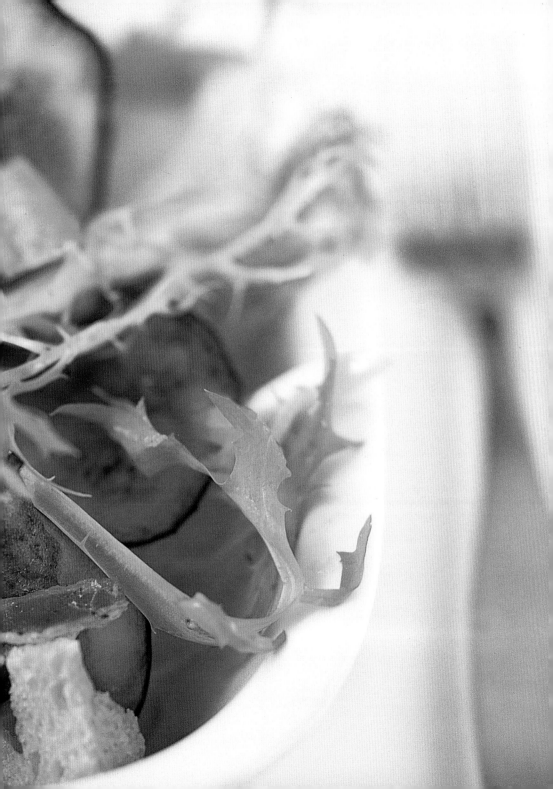

Endive, pancetta, and eggplant salad

Illustrated on previous pages

¼ pound sliced smoked pancetta, derinded

4 tablespoons olive oil

4 slices white bread, crusts removed, cut into cubes

2 garlic cloves, crushed

vegetable oil, for deep-frying

1 eggplant, thinly sliced

¼ pound endive leaves

For the dressing

6 tablespoons extra virgin olive oil

1½ tablespoons balsamic vinegar

salt and pepper

1 Broil the pancetta for 2–3 minutes each side until crisp and golden. Cool, then crumble into bite-size pieces.

2 Heat the olive oil in a skillet. Fry the bread cubes for a few minutes until golden all over, adding the garlic for the last minute. Drain on paper towels.

3 Heat a 2-inch depth of oil in a heavy pan to 310°F. Deep-fry the eggplant slices in batches for 1–2 minutes until crisp. Drain on paper towels; keep warm in the oven.

4 Put the endive in a large bowl and add the bacon and croûtons. Whisk the dressing ingredients together, then pour over the salad and toss lightly. Serve in individual bowls, topped with the eggplant chips.

Note Smoked pancetta is available from Italian delicatessens and selected supermarkets. If unobtainable, use lightly smoked bacon instead.

Crisp fried eggplant slices add a new dimension to this classic salad.

Couscous salad with apricots and almonds

1¼ cups couscous
large pinch of saffron threads
1¼ cups hot vegetable stock
scant ⅓ cup ready-to-eat dried
  apricots, chopped
scant ½ cup raisins
3 tablespoons chopped fresh mint
3 tablespoons chopped fresh flat leaf
  parsley

finely grated zest of 1 lemon
3 tablespoons extra-virgin olive oil
salt and pepper
squeeze of lemon juice, to taste
2 tablespoons slivered almonds,
  toasted

1 Put the couscous into a bowl, add the saffron threads, then pour on the hot stock and leave to absorb for 10 minutes.

2 Add the apricots and raisins to the warm couscous, fork through, and set aside until cool.

3 When cold, add the chopped mint and parsley, grated lemon zest, and olive oil. Season with salt and pepper to taste, and toss to mix. Finish with a generous squeeze of lemon juice. Scatter with the toasted almonds to serve.

Variation For a more lemony flavor, add 1½ ounces chopped preserved lemon with the herbs.

This fruity couscous salad can be prepared in advance and kept in the fridge, but bring it back to room temperature to serve.

Shredded cabbage with fruit and pistachios

Illustrated on previous pages

Serves 4–6

1¼ pounds white cabbage, cored and
   finely shredded
1 yellow grapefruit
1 pink grapefruit
1 orange
⅝ cup raisins (preferably large semi-
   dried raisins)

1 small bunch fresh chives, snipped
1 tablespoon walnut oil
salt and pepper
⅓ cup shelled roasted salted
   pistachio nuts, roughly chopped

1 Place the shredded cabbage in a large bowl.
2 Cut away all the skin and white pith from the grapefruit and orange, then, with a sharp knife, carefully cut the flesh from between the membranes. Do this over the bowl of cabbage, to catch the citrus juices.
3 Add the raisins, chives, oil, and seasoning; toss gently together.
4 Just before serving, toss in the chopped pistachio nuts.

A wonderfully refreshing, juicy salad—colorful enough to tempt even the most jaded of palates.

Zucchini, cucumber, and arugula salad

4 medium zucchini
6-inch piece cucumber, diced
¼ pound arugula leaves
salt and pepper
extra-virgin olive oil, for drizzling

1 Coarsely grate the zucchini, using a hand grater or a food processor fitted with a coarse grating disk. Turn into a bowl.
2 Add the cucumber to the zuccini and toss to mix. Add the arugula leaves, and toss carefully. Season with salt and pepper.
3 Arrange the salad in a shallow bowl, and drizzle with olive oil to serve.

Simply dressed with olive oil, so as not to disguise the delicate flavors, this fresh tasting salad is great with chicken or fish.

Belgian endive, radish, and onion salad

Illustrated on previous pages

4 bulbs of Belgian endive, cut into
  chunks
10–12 red salad radishes, quartered
1 red onion, very finely sliced

For the dressing
1 bunch watercress, stalks removed
4 tablespoons extra-virgin olive oil
1 tablespoons white wine vinegar
1 teaspoons black peppercorns
salt

1 Put the salad ingredients in a bowl of iced water while making the dressing.
2 Process the watercress leaves, oil, vinegar, and black peppercorns in a
blender or food processor until almost smooth. Taste and season with salt—
it should be quite peppery.
3 Drain and dry vegetables. Toss with half of the dressing, and then place
in a salad bowl. Drizzle with remaining dressing to serve.

A crunchy salad with a vivid green, peppery
dressing of puréed watercress.

New potato salad with chervil and chives

/1½ pounds new potatoes, scrubbed
salt and pepper
4 tablespoons mayonnaise
2 tablespoons Greek yogurt
1 teaspoon wholegrain mustard
2 tablespoons chopped fresh chervil

or flat leaf parsley
2 tablespoons chopped fresh chives
squeeze of lemon juice

1 Add the new potatoes to a pan of cold salted water, bring to the boil, and simmer for 12–15 minutes until just tender.

2 Meanwhile, combine the mayonnaise and yogurt in a large bowl and stir in the mustard. Season with salt and pepper to taste.

3 Drain the potatoes in a colander and cool slightly, then toss with the dressing and chopped herbs while still warm. Add a squeeze of lemon juice, and check the seasoning. Serve warm or at room temperature.

Chervil is a delicately flavored herb that goes well with potatoes; if unobtainable, simply use flat leaf parsley instead.

Baby beets with orange and walnuts

16 baby beets with leaves
4 oranges
4 tablespoons olive oil
salt and pepper
¾ cup walnut halves

1 Preheat oven to 375°F. Cut the tops from the beets; set aside. Scrub the beets and put in a baking dish.

2 Finely grate the rind from 2 oranges and squeeze the juice. Add this rind and juice to the beets with half the olive oil and the seasoning; toss to coat. Cover with foil, and bake for 45 minutes or until tender.

3 Meanwhile, peel and segment the remaining oranges, discarding all of the membrane and seeds.

4 Heat the remaining oil in a skillet, and add the beet tops. Sauté for 2–3 minutes until wilted and tender. Stir in the orange segments and walnuts. Season generously with salt and pepper.

5 Add the baked beets to the wilted beet tops. Toss to mix well and then serve immediately.

Young beets—bought in bunches—are best baked to retain all their earthy flavor. Combined with orange, walnuts, and their leafy tops, they make a heartwarming dish.

Spiced roast potatoes with garlic

2½ pounds potatoes, peeled and cut into 2-inch chunks
2 tablespoons all-purpose flour
1 tablespoon smoked paprika or mustard powder
1 teaspoon salt

4 tablespoons vegetable oil
2 garlic bulbs, cloves separated (unpeeled)

1 Preheat oven to 425°F. Put the potatoes in a large pan and add cold water to cover. Bring to the boil and boil steadily for 5 minutes. Immediately drain, and leave, uncovered, to cool slightly.

2 Mix together the flour, paprika or mustard, and salt. Put oil in a roasting pan and heat in the oven for a minute or two.

3 Meanwhile, toss the potato chunks in the spice mix to coat well. Carefully add to the hot oil, with the garlic cloves. Roast in the oven for 40–50 minutes until the potatoes are crunchy and browned, turning halfway through cooking. Serve piping hot.

Potato cubes, tossed in smoked paprika or mustard powder and roasted in olive oil with whole garlic cloves for a tasty accompaniment.

Mashed potatoes with horseradish

2 pounds floury potatoes, peeled and
   cut into chunks
salt and pepper
scant 1 cup sour cream
2 tablespoons grated hot horseradish
1 tablespoon olive oil or butter

1 Add the potatoes to a large pan of cold salted water, bring to the boil,
and boil for 15–20 minutes until very tender.
2 Drain well, then shake the potatoes in the covered pan to drive off
moisture. Let rest in the pan, loosely covered, for a few minutes.
3 Meanwhile warm the cream, horseradish, and oil or butter together
in a small pan.
4 Mash the potatoes with the horseradish cream until smooth. Season
and serve.

This tasty mash is delicious served topped
with fried breadcrumbs spiked with extra
grated horseradish.

Roasted squash with shallots

2 butternut squash, each about
  1 pound
4 tablespoons butter
3 tablespoons maple syrup
12 shallots, peeled

12 garlic cloves (unpeeled)
2 tablespoons raisins
salt and pepper

1 Preheat oven to 400°F. Halve the squash, scoop out the seeds, then peel. Cut the flesh into large chunks.
2 Melt the butter with the maple syrup in a roasting dish. Add the shallots and squash, toss to coat, and bake for 20 minutes.
3 Add the garlic cloves and raisins and bake for a further 20 minutes or until the squash and garlic are tender and beginning to caramelize. Season generously and serve.

Sweet butternut squash, enriched with caramelized shallots and earthy roast garlic. Serve with roast pork, turkey, or duck.

Roasted tomatoes and pepper salad

Illustrated on previous pages

2 red bell peppers, halved, cored, and seeded

2 yellow bell peppers, halved, cored, and seeded

6 tablespoons olive oil

6 ripe plum tomatoes, quartered and cored

12 large garlic cloves (unpeeled)

2 tablespoons balsamic vinegar

salt and pepper

1 Preheat oven to 400°F. Cut each pepper half into 3 or 4 thick strips. Toss with the olive oil and place on a baking tray. Bake for 15 minutes.

2 Stir in the tomatoes and unpeeled garlic cloves, and roast for another 15–20 minutes or until the garlic cloves are soft and the peppers begin to color.

3 Lift out the roasted vegetables and garlic with a slotted spoon, and place in a warm serving dish. Swirl the balsamic vinegar into the pan juices. Bring to the boil and let bubble for 30 seconds, then pour over the tomatoes and peppers.

4 Season with salt and pepper to taste, and serve immediately, or allow to cool to room temperature; do not refrigerate.

A gutsy, colorful cooked salad inspired by the flavors of the Mediterranean. Serve as an accompaniment to broiled meat.

Hasselback potatoes

8 even sized, slightly oval potatoes,
    each about 5 ounces
2 tablespoons truffle oil, or extra-
    virgin olive oil
1 small bunch fresh thyme
coarse salt

1 Preheat oven to 425°F. Slice each potato vertically across its width at
⅛-inch intervals, without cutting right through. Rinse, then put the potatoes
in a bowl of chilled water for 15 minutes; they will open out slightly. Drain
and dry well.
2 Brush the oil between the potato slices and all over the skin. Push a small
thyme sprig into each slit. Season with salt.
3 Place each potato on an 8-inch square of foil, pull up the corners, and
twist loosely. Put the parcels on a baking sheet, and bake in the oven for
40 minutes. Fold back the foil slightly and bake for another 30–40 minutes
until the potatoes are cooked.

These thyme-scented, fanned roast potatoes
are excellent with poultry and game.

Bok choi with shiitake mushrooms

1¼ pounds bok choi, stems removed
2 tablespoons vegetable oil
3 large garlic cloves, finely sliced
6 green onions, finely sliced
¾ pound shiitake mushrooms, thickly sliced
½ teaspoon coarsely ground black pepper

1½ tablespoons superfine sugar
1 teaspoon sesame oil
1 tablespoon rice wine or rice wine vinegar
3 tablespoons dark soy sauce

To serve
sesame oil, for drizzling (optional)

1 Separate and roughly chop the bok choi leaves. Add to a large pan of boiling water, and cook for 2 minutes; drain thoroughly and set aside.

2 Heat the oil in a large wok. Add the garlic, green onions, mushrooms, and pepper, and stir-fry for 4–5 minutes.

3 Add the sugar, sesame oil, rice wine, and soy sauce. Stir-fry for 2 minutes, then add the blanched bok choi, toss well, and heat through.

4 Serve at once in warmed bowls, drizzled with a little sesame oil, if wished, and accompanied by rice or noodles.

Quick and easy Chinese stir-fried vegetables, flavored with soy, sesame, and rice wine.

Potato and celeriac rösti

1½ pounds floury potatoes
salt and pepper
1 large celeriac (approx. ¾ pound),
   peeled

1–2 teaspoons fennel seeds (optional)
2 tablespoons olive oil
4 tablespoons butter

1 Put the unpeeled potatoes in a large pan of cold salted water with the celeriac. Bring to the boil and parboil for about 8–10 minutes. Drain; leave until cool enough to handle, then peel the potatoes.

2 Coarsely grate the potatoes and celeriac into a large bowl, and toss in the fennel seeds if using; mix well. Season with salt and pepper to taste.

3 Heat 1 tablespoon of the oil in a 9-inch sauté pan, and add half of the butter. When melted and foaming, tip in the potato mixture and spread evenly; don't press down too firmly. Cook over a moderate heat for about 15 minutes, shaking the pan from time to time to prevent the rösti from sticking.

4 Invert a plate over the pan, then turn the rösti out onto the plate. Add the remaining oil and butter to pan and heat until foaming. Slide the rösti back into the pan, and fry the uncooked side for 15–20 minutes, shaking the pan occasionally. Serve cut into wedges.

An excellent accompaniment to poultry and game, especially chicken and duck breasts.

Zucchini, chile and sugar-snap sauté

3 tablespoons olive oil
4 medium zucchini, cut into broad
strips
6 ounces sugar-snap peas
1 plump green chile, halved, seeded,
and minced

2 tablespoons sour cream
3 tablespoons chopped fresh cilantro
salt and pepper

1 Heat the oil in a skillet or sauté pan, and add the zucchini and sugar-snaps. Stir-fry for 3 minutes, then add the chile and stir for 1 minute. Remove from the heat.
2 Stir in the sour cream and cilantro. Season and serve at once.

A fast stir-fry of green vegetables with a hint of chile, enriched with a little sour cream.

Peas with cherry tomatoes and spinach

Illustrated on previous pages

1½ cups shelled fresh or frozen peas
⅝ cup dry white wine
2 tablespoons olive oil
1–2 fresh bay leaves
6 ounces whole ripe cherry tomatoes

½ pound fresh leaf spinach, stalks
  removed (see note)
salt and pepper

1 Place the peas in a large pan with the wine, olive oil, and bay leaves. Bring to the boil, then lower the heat and simmer gently for 5 minutes.
2 Add the cherry tomatoes, and simmer for another 5 minutes until tender and the liquid is well reduced.
3 Finally, stir in the spinach, and cook for a few minutes, turning occasionally, until the leaves just wilt.
4 Season with salt and pepper to taste. Serve immediately.

Note For convenience, buy bags of ready-prepared spinach from supermarkets. Otherwise, choose small, tender spinach leaves, and wash thoroughly in several changes of water to remove all traces of grit. Drain thoroughly before cooking.

This is a sort of quick vegetable stew—very colorful and full of goodness! Serve with broiled or roast poultry or other meat.

Moroccan spiced cauliflower with mint

Serves 4–6

1 medium cauliflower, divided into
   florets
6 tablespoons butter
1 teaspoon sweet paprika
½ teaspoon ground cumin
½ teaspoon ground coriander
salt and pepper
handful of fresh mint leaves

1 Steam the cauliflower over boiling water for 10–12 minutes until just tender. Remove and allow to dry a little.
2 Melt the butter in a skillet. When sizzling, add the spices and fry, stirring, for 30 seconds. Add the cauliflower florets, and stir to coat with the buttery spices. Season well with salt and pepper.
3 Add the mint leaves, and cook gently until wilted. Serve immediately.

Cauliflower is lightly steamed until tender, then tossed in a Moroccan spiced melted butter with fresh mint leaves.

easy
desserts
and bakes

White chocolate and berry creams

1¼ pounds frozen mixed summer fruits (raspberries, blackberries, redcurrants, etc.)

3 tablespoons confectioners' sugar

4 teaspoons cassis, framboise, or kirsch

7 ounces white chocolate, in pieces

generous ½ cup whole milk raspberry yogurt

2 cups fromage blanc with added cream

white chocolate curls or grated chocolate, to decorate

1 Tip the frozen fruits into a bowl, stir in the confectioners' sugar, then spoon into 4 wide stemmed glasses and drizzle the liqueur over.

2 Put the chocolate in a large heatproof bowl over a pan of simmering water until just melted. Remove from the heat, then beat in the yogurt and fromage frais until smooth.

3 Spoon the chocolate mixture over the fruit, and leave in a cool place to allow the fruits to thaw slowly.

4 Serve topped with chocolate curls or grated chocolate.

Tart summer berries under a contrasting blanket of smooth, creamy white chocolate is an irresistible combination.

Amaretto and blueberry syllabubs

For the blueberry layer
2½ cups blueberries
1 tablespoon Amaretto liqueur
1 tablespoon superfine sugar
For the syllabub
scant 1¼ cups heavy cream
2 tablespoons superfine sugar

⅝ cup medium white wine, such as
  Riesling
3 tablespoons Amaretto liqueur
8 amaretti cookies, broken into small
  pieces
To decorate
mint leaves

1 Tip the blueberries into a large pan. Add the liqueur and sugar, and poach gently for 1–2 minutes until the berries have softened, but have not burst. Allow to cool.

2 To make the syllabub, pour the cream into a bowl. Add the sugar, wine, and liqueur, and whisk until the mixture holds its shape.

3 Toss the blueberries with the amaretti biscuits, then layer with the creamy syllabub in 4 stemmed glasses. Chill until required.

4 Serve the chilled syllabubs decorated with mint leaves.

Note Fresh gooseberries, apricots, and plums all make excellent alternatives to blueberries. Stone and quarter plums or apricots. Adjust the sugar accordingly, and poach until the fruit is tender, but still retaining shape.

Topped with an almond flavored syllabub, poached blueberries make an elegant, quick dessert—ideal for mid-week entertaining.

Pan-fried banana with orange and cardamom

4 tablespoons unsalted butter
⅓ cup light muscovado sugar
5 cardamom pods, lightly crushed
4 bananas, peeled and halved
    lengthwise
grated rind and juice of 1 large
    orange

1 Melt the butter in a large skillet, then add the sugar with the cardamom, and stir until the sugar is dissolved.
2 Add the bananas, and cook for 1–2 minutes, turning them in the juices, until softened. Add the orange juice and rind and let bubble until reduced and syrupy. Discard the cardamon pods.
3 Serve hot, with vanilla ice cream.

Cardamom adds an exotic flavor to this hot dessert. Vanilla ice cream is the perfect accompaniment.

Caramelized apples on brioche toasts

3 tablespoons sugar
3 well flavored eating apples, peeled, cored, and thickly sliced
2 tablespoons butter
large pinch of ground cinnamon
3 tablespoons raisins

juice of 1 lemon
4 thick slices of brioche (from a large brioche loaf)
1 cup Greek yogurt

1 Sprinkle the sugar over the base of a large skillet, and heat gently until it melts and begins to caramelize—don't allow to darken.
2 Add the apples and toss to coat, then add the butter, cinnamon, raisins, lemon juice, and 1 tablespoon water. Cook, turning frequently, for 1–2 minutes.
3 Meanwhile, toast the brioche slices under a hot broiler until golden on both sides. Place on serving plates.
4 Spoon the yogurt onto the brioche, and top with the caramelized apples and pan juices to serve.

Butter-enriched brioche makes a delicious base for pan-fried apple slices.

Plum and hazelnut streusel cake

8–10 slices

1⅜ cup self-rising flour

1½ teaspoon baking powder

1 teaspoon ground cinnamon

1¼ sticks unsalted butter, softened

⅝ cup superfine sugar

3 large eggs, beaten

1 cup ground hazelnuts

6–8 plums, halved and stoned

For the streusel topping

generous ⅛ cup all-purpose flour

¼ cup rolled oats

2 tablespoons chilled butter, finely diced

generous ¼ cup light muscovado sugar

scant ½ cup hazelnuts, roughly chopped

1 Preheat oven to 350°F. Grease and base line a 10x8-inch baking pan. Sift the flour with the baking powder and the cinnamon.

2 Cream the butter and sugar together in a bowl until pale and fluffy, then gradually beat in the eggs, adding a little of the flour with the last of the egg, to prevent curdling.

3 Fold in the remaining flour mixture and ground nuts. Spoon into the prepared pan and level the surface.

4 Arrange the plums, cut side up, over the cake, pressing down gently. Mix the streusel ingredients together and scatter over the top.

5 Bake for 45–50 minutes until risen and lightly golden, and so that a skewer inserted into the center comes out hot. Leave in the tin for 10 minutes, then remove. Serve warm, with custard or crème fraîche.

Variation Use ground almonds instead of hazelnuts, and apricots in place of plums.

A warm cinnamon scented hazelnut cake, covered with fresh plum halves and topped with a rich nutty streusel.

Glazed mille-feuilles

8 small sheets filo pastry (each about 12x7 inches)
4 tablespoons butter, melted
8 tablespoons confectioners' sugar, sifted
¼ pound mascarpone
4 teaspoons rosewater essence

⅝ cup heavy cream
3 cups mixed berries, such as raspberries, strawberries, redcurrants, blueberries, and blackberries
mint leaves, to decorate (optional)

1 Preheat oven to 400°F. Lay a sheet of filo on a clean surface (keep the rest covered). Brush with melted butter, then layer 3 more sheets on top, brushing all except the top sheet with butter. Repeat to make another stack with remaining filo.

2 Cut each stack into 6 triangles; it won't matter if they are a little uneven. Place on baking sheets, and dust with approximately 2 tablespoons of the confectioners' sugar. Bake for 10–12 minutes until crisp and golden.

3 Pop under a hot broiler (not too close to the element) for 15–30 seconds to glaze. Transfer to a wire rack to cool.

4 For the filling, beat the mascarpone with 4 tablespoons confectioners' sugar and the rosewater until smooth. Lightly whip the cream in another bowl, then gently fold into the mascarpone.

5 To assemble, layer 3 filo triangles per serving with mascarpone cream and fruit. Top with a sprig of redcurrants, and mint leaves if using. Just before serving, dust with the remaining confectioners' sugar.

Note For convenience, prepare ahead to the end of stage 4. Assemble the mille feuilles 2 hours before serving.

These impressive filo stacks—layered with mascarpone and berries—are deceptively easy.

Melon, mint, and ginger compote

Serves 8

1 medium Galia melon
1 cantaloupe melon
¼ small watermelon
1-inch piece fresh gingerroot, peeled
   and roughly chopped

1 tablespoon freshly torn mint leaves
rosemary flowers or mint sprigs,
   to decorate

1 Halve the whole melons. Scoop out the seeds from all 3 melons, then cut the flesh into chunks and place in a large bowl, adding any juices.

2 Put the ginger in a clean garlic press, hold over the melon bowl, and press firmly, to extract the ginger juice. Add the mint leaves and toss gently. Chill until required.

3 Just before serving, toss lightly and scatter with some rosemary flowers or mint sprigs.

A refreshing, healthy fruit salad with the zing of freshly pressed ginger. Perfectly ripe melons are essential.

Peaches in elderflower champagne

Serves 6–8

6–8 peaches, ripe but firm

½ cup elderflower cordial

½ bottle dry Champagne or other
good-quality sparkling white wine

1 Preheat oven to 400°F. Arrange the peaches closely in a deep ovenproof
dish (just large enough to hold them in a single layer).

2 Measure the elderflower cordial into a jug, add the Champagne or
sparkling wine, then pour the mixture over the peaches. Cover the dish
with a lid, or with waxed paper, then a layer of foil to seal.

3 Bake for 40–50 minutes, or until the peaches are tender right through. If
they are not fully submerged in the liquid, turn them over halfway through
the cooking time.

4 Leave the peaches to cool in the syrup. If preferred, lift out and peel off the
skins, then return the peaches to the elderflower Champagne to serve.

Luxuriously steeped in Champagne sweetened
with a little elderflower cordial, these peaches
make a mouthwatering summer dessert.

Raspberry yoghurt ice

Serves 4–6

2 pounds 2 ounces raspberries

2 tablespoons light muscovado sugar

6 tablespoons maple syrup

2¼ cups organic yogurt

1 Put the raspberries and sugar in a blender or food processor, and mix to a purée, then pass through a sieve into a bowl to remove the seeds.

2 Stir the maple syrup and yogurt into the raspberry purée.

3 Freeze in an ice cream maker, if you have one, according to the manufacturer's instructions. Alternatively, pour the fruit mixture into a freezerproof container, and place in the coldest part of the freezer until partially frozen. As the ice crystals begin to form around the edges, remove the container from the freezer, and whisk the raspberry mixture to break up the ice crystals. Return to the freezer. Repeat this process once more, then freeze until firm.

4 If necessary, transfer the yogurt ice to the fridge 30 minutes before serving, to soften.

This wonderfully fresh-tasting ice relies on the use of flavorful, ripe raspberries.

Strawberry yoghurt ice

Serves 4–6

⅝ cup superfine sugar

¾ cup water

2 pounds 2 ounces strawberries

2¼ cups organic yogurt

1 Dissolve the sugar in the water in a small pan over a low heat. Increase the heat, bring to the boil, and boil steadily until the syrup registers 225°F on a candy thermometer. Allow to cool.

2 Put the strawberries in a blender or food processor, and mix to a purée, then pass through a sieve into a bowl to remove the seeds. Stir in the sugar syrup, followed by the yogurt.

3 Freeze in an ice cream maker if you have one, according to the manufacturer's instructions. Alternatively, pour the fruit mixture into a freezerproof container and place in the coldest part of the freezer until partially frozen. As the ice crystals begin to form around the edges, remove the container from the freezer, and whizz the strawberry mixture to break up the ice crystals. Return to the freezer. Repeat this process once more, then freeze until firm.

4 If necessary, transfer the strawberry yogurt ice to the fridge approximately 30 minutes before serving to soften.

Make this refreshing ice during the summer, when fragrant, homegrown strawberries are available.

Lime and papaya posset

Serves 6
2½ cups heavy cream
¾ cup superfine sugar
finely grated rind of 1 lime
juice of 2 limes
2 papayas, peeled, seeded, and
　chopped

1 Put the cream and sugar in a pan, heat gently until the sugar is dissolved, then boil for 3 minutes. Add half of the lime rind and all of the lime juice; stir well. Leave to cool for about 10 minutes.
2 Set aside 6 pieces of papaya; divide the rest between 6 individual glass bowls, then pour the lime mixture on top. Top with the lime rind and reserved papaya. Chill until ready to serve.

Note Perfectly ripe papayas are essential for this dessert.

Papaya has a special affinity with lime and the combination works beautifully in this dessert.

Triple chocolate brownies

Illustrated on previous pages

Makes about 12

1 stick (8 tablespoons) butter, plus extra for greasing

3 ounces good-quality dark chocolate (minimum 70% cocoa solids), in pieces

4 medium eggs, beaten

2 teaspoons vanilla extract

1¾ cup superfine sugar

generous ¾ cup all-purpose flour

generous ⅛ cup cocoa powder

115g packet milk chocolate chips

¾ cup white chocolate chips

8 butterscotch, roughly chopped

1 Preheat oven to 375°F. Liberally butter a shallow 11x7-inch baking pan and then line the base with nonstick baking parchment.

2 Melt the butter with the chocolate in a doubler boiler over simmering water. Remove from heat, and stir in the beaten eggs, vanilla extract, and sugar. Mix thoroughly.

3 Sift the flour with the cocoa powder over the mixture, then beat in until evenly incorporated. Stir in the chocolate chips and butterscotch pieces.

4 Spoon the mixture into the pan and spread evenly. Bake in the middle of the oven for about 35 minutes until set, but still moist. Leave to cool in the pan.

5 Turn out when completely cold, and cut into squares or bars to serve.

Note These delicious chocolate brownies have the characteristic fudge-like texture. For a more cakelike texture, bake for an extra 5–10 minutes.

These irresistible rich, moist dark chocolate brownies are laden with milk and white chocolate chips and butterscotch pieces.

Orange almond cake with rosewater cream

8–10 slices

6 large eggs, separated
¾ cup superfine sugar
grated rind of 2 oranges
juice of 1 orange
1⅜ cup ground almonds

For the rosewater cream

2 cardamom pods, seeds extracted
2 tablespoons rosewater essence
1 tablespoon superfine sugar
1¼ cup heavy cream

1 Preheat oven to 350°F. Grease and base line a 9-inch springform cake pan.

2 In a bowl, whisk the egg yolks, sugar, and orange rind together until pale and thick. Stir in the orange juice, then fold in the ground almonds.

3 In a clean bowl, whisk the egg whites until just peaking, then fold into the cake mixture.

4 Spoon into the prepared pan, and bake for 45–50 minutes until risen and firm to touch, covering loosely with foil after 20 minutes, if the cake appears to be over-browning.

5 Meanwhile, for the cream, lightly crush the cardamom seeds, and put in a small pan with the rosewater and sugar. Warm gently to dissolve the sugar. Allow to cool, then strain.

6 Whip the cream in a bowl, slowly adding the cooled syrup, until it forms soft peaks.

7 Serve the cake cut into wedges, accompanied by the rosewater cream.

A lovely light almond sponge cake with a hint of orange, accompanied by an exotic rosewater and cardamom cream.

Lemon polenta cake

8–10 slices

generous ¾ cup polenta (ordinary or
   quick-cook), plus extra for dusting
generous ¾ cup flour
1½ teaspoon baking powder
2 large eggs, plus 3 egg whites
¾ cup superfine sugar
grated rind of 2 lemons

½ cup lemon juice (juice of 2–3
   lemons)
1 vanilla bean, seeds extracted
½ cup vegetable oil
⅝ cup buttermilk

To serve (optional)
crème fraîche
strawberries

1 Preheat oven to 350°F. Grease and base line a 10-inch springform cake
pan. Dust the pan with a little polenta.

2 Sift the flour and the baking powder together into a bowl, then stir
in the polenta.

3 In a separate bowl, whisk the whole eggs, egg whites, and sugar together
until pale and thick.

4 Add the polenta mixture, lemon rind, and juice, vanilla seeds, oil, and
buttermilk. Carefully fold into the whisked mixture, using a large
metal spoon.

5 Spoon the mixture into the prepared pan and bake for 30 minutes, or until
a skewer inserted into the center comes out clean. Transfer to a wire rack
and leave to cool completely.

6 Cut into slices and serve with crème fraîche and strawberries, if you like.

Polenta colors this cake a pretty shade
of yellow and also adds a subtle crunch.
Fresh strawberries and crème fraîche are
the perfect complement.

Focaccia with figs and raisins

Serves 4–6

¾ cup seedless raisins
⅝ cup medium or sweet sherry
1 cup hand-hot water
2 teaspoons active dried yeast

10 ounces instant pizza mix
½ cup brown sugar
6–8 fresh figs, sliced
olive oil, for drizzling

1 Oil an 11x7-inch shallow baking pan. Put the raisins in a bowl. Warm the sherry, pour over the raisin and set aside to soak.

2 Pour the water into a bowl, sprinkle the yeast on, stir, and leave to froth for 15 minutes.

3 Put the pizza mix in a large bowl, stir in a generous ¼ cup of the sugar, and make a well in the center. Add the frothed yeast, and mix to a soft dough.

4 Turn out on to a floured surface, and knead for 2–3 minutes until smooth. Drain the raisins, reserving the liquid, then knead them into the dough.

5 Press into the prepared baking pan, pushing the dough to the edges. Cover with oiled plastic wrap and leave to rise in a warm place for about 30 minutes until doubled in height.

6 Preheat oven to 425°F. Make dimples all over the surface of the dough with your fingers, and lay the sliced figs on top. Drizzle with a little olive oil and sprinkle with the remaining sugar. Bake for 10–15 minutes until golden and caramelised.

7 Spoon the reserved sherry over the focaccia; cool slightly. Serve warm, with soft goat cheese or crème fraîche.

Topped with juicy caramelized figs, this soft sweet focaccia is made with pizza mix lightened with a little extra yeast.

Gingerbread with figs

16–20 slices
3¼ cups self-rising flour
½ teaspoon salt
½ teaspoon baking soda
2 teaspoons ground ginger
⅝ cup dried figs, chopped
¼ cup crystallized ginger, diced

1⅓ cup light muscovado sugar
1½ sticks butter
½ cup molasses
½ cup corn syrup
1¼ cup milk
2 medium eggs, beaten

1 Preheat oven to 350°F. Grease and line a 10-inch square cake pan.
2 Sift the flour, salt, baking soda, and ground ginger into a bowl. Stir in the figs and diced ginger. Make a well in the centre.
3 Put the sugar, butter, molasses, corn syrup, and milk in a pan, and heat gently until melted. Pour into the well, and add the eggs. Stir to mix, then beat for 1 minute.
4 Turn the mixture into the prepared pan and bake for 1–1¼ hours until a skewer inserted in the center comes out clean.
5 Leave in pan for 10 minutes, then transfer to a wire rack to cool. Serve cut into bans.

Jamaican style gingerbread flavored with chopped dried figs and crystallized ginger.

Cinnamon chocolate chip cookies

Illustrated on page 292

Makes 24

1¼ sticks (8 tablespoons) butter or
  margarine, softened
1⅛ cup soft brown sugar
scant ¼ cup superfine sugar
2 medium eggs, beaten
2½ cups all-purpose flour

1 teaspoon baking of soda
½ teaspoon salt
1 teaspoon ground cinnamon
1 cup chopped peanuts
1¼ cups chocolate chips

1 Preheat oven to 375°F. Cream the butter and sugars together in a bowl until soft and fluffy. Beat in the eggs.

2 Sift the flour, baking soda, salt, and cinnamon together over the mixture. Beat well, then stir in the peanuts and chocolate.

3 Drop tablespoonfuls of the mixture well apart onto baking sheets lined with nonstick baking parchment, and flatten slightly. Bake for 15–17 minutes until golden.

4 Leave on baking sheets for 10 minutes, then transfer cookies to a wire rack to cool.

Variation Shape smaller cookies if you prefer, reducing the cooking time by 2–3 minutes.

Giant cookies – crisp on the outside, yet meltingly soft within.

Lavender and ginger cookies

Illustrated on page 293

Makes about 36

1 stick butter, softened

⅜ cup superfine sugar

1 medium egg, beaten

1 teaspoon vanilla extract

1 tablespoon fresh or dried lavender flowers

1 tablespoon chopped preserved ginger

1⅜ cup all-purpose flour

¼ teaspoon baking soda

½ teaspoon each baking powder and salt

½ teaspoon ground ginger

¼ cup sour cream or crème fraîche

1 Cream the butter and sugar together in a bowl until soft. Beat in the egg, vanilla, and lavender, then fold in the chopped ginger.

2 Sift the flour with the baking soda, baking powder, salt, and ground ginger. Beat into the mixture, alternately with the sour cream; the dough will be quite soft.

3 Tip the dough onto a sheet of waxed paper, and gently roll into a cylinder, about 2 inches thick. Wrap tightly in plastic wrap and refrigerate for at least 6 hours, preferably overnight.

4 To bake, preheat oven to 375°F. Slice off thin disks from the dough as required. Place on baking sheets lined with nonstick baking parchment. Bake for 8–10 minutes until pale golden and set.

5 Cool slightly on the baking sheets, then transfer to a wire rack to cool.

Note If using dried lavender, buy a culinary grade—obtainable from herb suppliers, or dry your own flowers if you have lavender in the garden.

Exquisite fragrant cookies that can be freshly baked to order. Make the dough in advance, keep chilled, then slice and bake as required.

Carrot and raisin cookies

Illustrated on page 293

Makes about 36
2 cups freshly cooked carrots, thickly sliced
1 stick butter or margarine, softened
generous ¾ cup light muscovado sugar
1 large egg, beaten
scant 3 cups all-purpose flour
1½ teaspoon baking powder
½ teaspoon ground cinnamon
¼ teaspoon ground nutmeg
¼ teaspoon ground ginger
¼ teaspoon salt
1 cup seedless raisins
½ cup pecan nuts or walnuts, chopped

1 Preheat oven to 375°F. Line two baking sheets with nonstick baking parchment. Dry the carrots on paper towels, then mash thoroughly until smooth.
2 Cream the butter and sugar together in a bowl. Add the mashed carrot and egg.
3 Sift the flour, baking powder, spices, and salt over the mixture, then beat together thoroughly. Stir in the raisins and nuts.
4 Drop teaspoonfuls of the mixture onto the baking sheets, spacing well apart, then flatten the mixture with the back of a wet spoon to shape roughly into disks. Bake for 12–15 minutes until light golden brown.
5 Leave on the baking sheet for 10 minutes, then transfer to a wire rack to cool completely.

These lightly spiced drop cookies are perfect for lunch boxes.

Vanilla thins

Makes 36

generous 2 cups all-purpose flour
1 teaspoon baking powder
½ teaspoon salt
2 vanilla beans, split
2 sticks butter, cubed and softened
scant 1 cup superfine sugar
1 large egg, beaten

1 Sift flour with baking powder and salt onto a sheet of waxed paper.
2 Scrape the seeds from the vanilla beans into the food processor. Add the butter and sugar, and process until pale and fluffy. Add the egg and mix until incorporated.
3 Add the sifted flour and process briefly to a soft dough; do not overmix.
4 Turn onto a floured surface, and knead lightly. Lift onto waxed paper, and roll the dough into a cylinder, 2 inches thick. Wrap tightly in plastic wrap, and refrigerate for at least 6 hours, preferably overnight.
5 To bake, preheat oven to 375°F. Cut thin slices from the dough as required. Place on baking sheets lined with nonstick baking parchment; bake for about 10 minutes until golden and set. Cool slightly on baking sheets, then transfer to a wire rack to cool.

Note This cookie dough will keep tightly wrapped in the fridge for up to 1 week.

Flavored with real vanilla seeds, these delicate biscuits make an elegant treat to serve with coffee or ice cream.

Coconut and blueberry cupcakes

Makes 8

1 stick (8 tablespoons) unsalted
  butter, at room temperature
½ cup superfine sugar
2 tablespoons milk
2 large eggs, lightly beaten

scant ⅝ cup self-rising flour
½ teaspoon baking powder
1 cup coconut
generous 1 cup blueberries

1 Preheat oven to 350°F. Line a muffin tin with 8 paper baking cups.
2 Cream the butter and sugar together in a bowl until pale and fluffy, then stir in the milk. Beat in the eggs, a little at a time.
3 Sift the flour and baking powder together over the mixture, add the coconut, and fold in carefully. Gently fold in most of the blueberries and spoon into the baking cups.
4 Scatter the remaining blueberries on top and bake for 20–25 minutes until firm to the touch. Cool on a wire rack.

Deliciously moist, fruity cupcakes.

Index

Acknowledgments

The publishers wish to thank the following for the loan of props for photography:
The Conran Shop, Michelin House, 81 Fulham Road, London SW3 (0207 589 7401); **Divertimenti**, 139–141 Fulham Road, London SW3 (0207 581 8065); **Divertimenti**, 45–7 Wigmore Street, London W1 (0207 935 0689); **Designers Guild**, 277 Kings Road, London SW3 (0207 351 5775); **Habitat**, 196 Tottenham Court Road, London W1 (0207 631 3880); **Ikea**, Purley Way, Croydon (0208 208 5607); **Inventory**, 26–40 Kensington High Street, London W8 (0207 937 2626); **Jerry's**, 163–7 Fulham Road, London SW3 (0207 581 0909); **LSA International**, The Dolphin Estate, Windmill Road, Sunbury on Thames, Middlesex (01932 789 721); **Muji**, 26 Great Marlborough Street, London W1 (0207 494 1197)

Food Stylists Maxine Clark, Joanna Farrow, Marie Ange Lapierre, Louise Pickford, Bridget Sargeson, Linda Tubby
Photographic Stylists Kasha Harmer Hirst, Maya Babic
Contributors Sara Buenfeld, Maxine Clark, Joanna Farrow, Janet Illsley, Louise Pickford, Bridget Sargeson, Linda Tubby, Sunil Vijayakar